蝦貝蟹

SHELLFISH

CHINESE STYLE MADE EASY

Mariscos Estilo Chino Fácil de Preparar

味全食譜
Wei-Chuan Cookbook

編輯
黃淑惠

食譜提供
李木村
許文舜
洪柏惟
伍　明
林茂盛

文稿協助
林淑華
賴燕真
何久恩
李愛茜
陳常彥
黃穎新
馬利亞
陳素真
蔡壽蓮

英文翻譯
蕭杏如

西文翻譯
安保羅
安西雅

設計編輯
張方馨
汪金光

封面設計
王　瑾

攝影
章靄琳
大野現
林坤鴻

電腦排版
錦龍印刷實業股份有限公司
分色製版輸出
尚品彩色製版印刷股份有限公司
印刷
錦龍印刷實業股份有限公司

味全出版社有限公司
台北市仁愛路四段28號2樓
電話：2702-1148．2702-1149
傳真：2704-2729
郵政劃撥00182038號
味全出版社帳戶

版權所有：
局版台業字第0179號
中華民國87年2月初版
定價：新台幣參佰元整

Editor
Su-Huei Huang

Recipes
Mu-Tsun Lee
Wen-Shun Hsu
Po-Wei Hung
Ming Wu
Mao-Sheng Lin

Editorial Staff
Sophia Lin
Yen Jen Lai
John Holt
Elsa Lee
Chang-Yen C. Shen
Vincent Wong
Maria Teresa Aguirre
Su Jen Chen
Shou Lien Tsai

English Translation
Bernadette Hsin Burkhead

Spanish Translation
Paul Andersen
Sylvia Jimenez-Andersen

Art Direction
F.S. Chang
Chin-Kuang Wang

Cover Design
Chin Ong

Photography
Irene Chang
Aki Ohno
Lin Kun Hon

PRINTED IN TAIWAN, R.O.C.
JIN LONG PRINTING & STATIONERY
CO.,LID

WEI-CHUAN PUBLISHING
1455 Monterey Pass Road, #110
Monterey Park, CA 91754, U.S.A.
Tel: 213-261-3880
Fax: 213-261-3299

FIRST PRINTING, FEBRUARY 1998
ISBN 0-941676-73-0
(English/Chinese/Spanish)

Editor
Huang Su-Huei

Recetas
Mu-Tsun Lee
Wen-Shun Hsu
Po-Wei Huang
Ming Wu
Mao-Sheng Lin

Asistentes del Editor
Sophia Lin
Yen Jen Lai
John Holt
Elsa Lee
Chang-Yen C. Shen
Vincent Wong
Maria Teresa Aguirre
Su Jen Chen
Shou Lien Tsai

Traducción al Inglés
Bernadette Hsin Burkhead

Traducción al Español
Paul Andersen
Sylvia Jiménez Andersen

Dirección Artística
F.S. Chang
Chin-Kuang Wang

Diseño de la Portada
Chin Ong

Fotografía
Irene Chang
Aki Ohno
Lin Kun Hon

Impreso en Taiwán, R.O.C.
*JIN LONG PRINTING &
STATIONERY CO.,LID*

Wei-Chuan Publishing
1455 Monterey Pass Road, #110
Monterey Park, CA 91754, U.S.A.
Tel: 213-261-3880
Fax: 213-261-3299

Wei-Chuan Cooking School was founded in 1961 as a subsidiary of Wei-Chuan Food Corporation, the largest food manufacturer in Taiwan. The school soon became the largest and most respected institution of its kind along the Asia-Pacific rim. Graduates include world-class chefs, institutional teachers, professional caterers, connoisseurs of Chinese and international cuisines as well as many homemakers.

As Wei-Chuan's reputation grew, requests came from all over the world for guidance and information relative to the recipes used in the cooking classes. In an effort to meet this demand, **Chinese Cuisine** was written and published in 1972. The book was very successful and became the first in a series of Wei-Chuan Cookbooks. Wei-Chuan Publishing was founded later that same year in Taipei with a branch subsequently established in the U.S.A. in 1978.

Wei-Chuan, long recognized as publishing the most comprehensive Chinese cuisine cookbooks, has now expanded its recipes to include other cuisines from around the world.

Wei-Chuan's success can be attributed to its commitment to provide the best quality product possible. All recipes are complemented by full color photographs. Each recipe is written simply with easy-to-follow instructions and precisely measured ingredients. Wei-Chuan stands behind its name, reputation, and commitment to remain true to the authenticity of its recipes.

La Escuela de Cocina Wei-Chuan fue fundada en 1961 como subsidiaria de Wei-Chuan Food Corporation, fabricante de comida más grande en Taiwán. La escuela pronto se convirtió en la institución más grande y respetada de su clase en el aro del Pacífico-Asiático. Nuestros graduados incluyen chefs reconocidos mundialmente, profesores institucionales, abastecedores profesionales y conocedores de cocina china como también amas de casa.

Mientras la reputación de Wei-Chuan creció, se recibían solicitudes de todas partes del mundo pidiendo consejos e información pertinentes a las recetas usadas en las clases de cocina. En un esfuerzo para satisfacer este requerimiento, Chinese Cuisine fue escrito y publicado en 1972. El libro fue un gran éxito y el primero en una serie de Libros de Cocina de Wei-Chuan. La casa editorial Wei-Chuan fue fundada, luego ese mismo año en Taipeh, seguida por una sucursal establecida en E.U. en 1978.

Los libros de cocina Wei-Chuan ahora se reconocen como los libros más completos en el campo de la cocina china. Los proyectos presentes de Wei-Chuan incluyen nuevos libros que cubren la cocina de todo el mundo.

El éxito de Wei-Chuan se debe a su compromiso en proveer el producto de más alta calidad posible. Casi todas las recetas se complementan con fotografías a todo color. Cada receta está escrita con instrucciones fáciles de seguir y con ingredientes meticulosamente medidos. Wei-Chuan respalda su nombre, su reputación y su compromiso en mantenerse fiel a la autenticidad de sus recetas.

Table of Contents　目　　　録　*Contenido*

Conversion Table · 量器介紹 · *Tabla de Conversión*

1 cup (1 c.) = 236 c.c
1杯(1飯碗)=16大匙   *taza(tz)·*

1 tablespoon (1 T.) = 15 c.c.
1大匙(1湯匙)   *cucharada (C.)*

1 teaspoon (1 t.) = 5 c.c.
1小匙(1茶匙)   *cucharadita (c.)*

序 味全原"海鮮專輯"是由李木村先生將其平日所蒐集的各式海鮮精華，加上海霸王、海村、珍寶等三家台灣著名的海鮮餐廳名廚：許文舜、洪柏惟、伍明及林茂盛先生所提供的資料編輯而成。

本書"蝦貝蟹"取材自味全原"海鮮專輯"，再加入李木村先生新增簡易的蝦貝蟹菜餚重新編輯整理後以全新面貌出版，希望對喜愛品嚐海鮮的讀者們能有所貢獻。

書內所使用的主料、配料（蔬菜）份量，除特別說明外均為處理過的淨重。

本食譜份量大部份為二人份，擬定二人份菜單時，可挑選一道海鮮，再另配一道菜與飯配食，講究者可多加前菜、湯或點心等。

涼拌、烤或炸類菜餚，可用來當前菜。

書內較特殊或製作複雜的菜餚列為宴客菜，份量為10人份，是以一桌酒席有10道菜餚，可供10個人食用計算，並非指一道菜供10個人食用。

Introduction
This new publication offers a fresh collection of seafood favorites from the famous teacher and chef Mu-Tsun Lee, who authored the popular best seller "Chinese Seafood". In addition, those shellfish recipes provided by Taiwan's most famous seafood restaurants "Hai Pa Wang", "Hai Tsun" and "Jumbo" in the original "Chinese Seafood" cookbook have been incorporated into this new book. The dishes presented here are certain to meet the highest expectations of the most discriminating seafood lovers.

The weights of the seafood and vegetables listed in this book are measured after being cleaned and/or filleted, etc. unless otherwise noted.

Most of the recipes in this book are made to serve two people. When preparing a meal for two, pick one seafood dish from the book then simply add one more dish and serve with rice. Appetizers, soup or dessert may be added as desired.

A cold, baked, or deep-fried dish may be used as an appetizer.

There are some unique and complex cooking recipes in the book, intended to serve 10 people. These are meant for formal dinner parties which include ten different dishes to be shared by each person.

When stir-frying or frying seafood or meat, always heat the wok then add oil to prevent sticking. If a non-stick pan is used, there is no need to heat the pan before adding oil.

Introducción
Esta nueva publicación ofrece una colección fresca de mariscos populares del famoso maestro y chef Mu-Tsun Lee, quien escribió el popular best seller "Chinese Seafood". Además, esas recetas de mariscos ofrecidas por los restaurantes más famosos de Taiwán: "Hai Pa Wang", "Hai Tsun" y "Jumbo" aparecen en el libro original "Chinese Seafood" y ahora han sido incorporadas a este nuevo libro. Indudablemente, esta cocina satisfará las mayores expectaciones de los más exigentes aficionados al pescado.

Las medidas de los mariscos y vegetales anotadas en este libro están calculadas después de haber sido limpiados y/o cortados en filetes, etc. a no ser que se especifique lo contrario.

La mayoría de las recetas en este libro sirve a dos personas. Cuando prepare un platillo para dos, escoja un platillo de mariscos de este libro y simplemente agregue otro platillo y sirva con arroz. Si lo desea, sirva con aperitivos, sopa, o postre.

Se puede usar como aperitivo, un platillo frío, horneado, o frito.

Hay algunas singulares y complejas recetas en este libro que tienen la intención de servir a 10 personas. Éstas son para meriendas formales, las cuales incluyen diez platillos diferentes para ser compartidos por cada persona.

Cuando fría-revolviendo o fría con bastante aceite mariscos o carne, siempre caliente la sartén wok y agregue aceite para que no se pegue la comida. Si usa una sartén en que no se pega la comida, no es necesario calentar la sartén antes de agregar el aceite.

Preparación de Camarones

1. **帶殼蝦**　順著蝦背剪開挑去腸泥。少鹽抓洗沖淨瀝乾後，拭乾水份，洒上太白粉以免油爆。(帶殼蝦料理見 10,12,20,22,23,24 頁)

2. **蝦仁**　先剝去殼，在蝦背輕劃刀，抽去腸泥，再按蝦仁6兩加鹽半小匙，水1大匙的比例抓拌後沖洗拭乾 (蝦仁料理見11,14-19,21,34,35 頁)

3. 大的蝦仁可片開成二片使用。

4. 處理好的蝦依份量調味，並加蛋白（無亦可），攪拌至水份完全吸收，加太白粉拌勻後，再加少許油使蝦易炒開且避免粘鍋。生蝦可調理多量，分袋冰凍，隨時取用。

炒蝦仁要領

5. 先炒配料，如太乾酌加1大匙水翻炒撈出，其湯汁不要。

6. 炒蝦仁時，如火力不夠，宜將蝦攤開煎15秒，翻面煎至全部變色後加回配料及調味料。

1. **To prepare shrimp with shell** With kitchen shears, cut through shell along the outer curve then devein the shrimp. Rub shrimp with a pinch of salt; rinse; pat dry then coat with cornstarch to prevent oil splatter during frying. (See pp. 10, 12, 20, 22, 23, 24 for recipes.)

2. **To prepare shelled shrimp** Shell the shrimp. Slit along the outer curve to expose the dark vein; devein. Rub 1/2 lb. (225g) shrimp with 1/2 t. salt and 1 T. water; rinse and drain. (See pp. 11, 14-19, 21, 34, 35 for recipes.)

3. If the shrimp is large, slice in half.

4. Season shrimp according to quantity of shrimp used, then add egg white (optional), mix well until water is absorbed completely. Add cornstarch; mix well. Mix in oil to separate shrimp easily during frying. Shrimp can be prepared and frozen in several bags for later use.

Tips for stir-frying shrimp

5. If accompanying ingredients are too dry when stir-frying, add 1 T. water. Stir-fry then remove; discard the liquid.

6. If heat is not high enough to stir-fry, spread shrimp out; pan-fry 15 seconds; turn shrimp over; fry until shrimp change color on all sides, then return the fried ingredients and add seasoning.

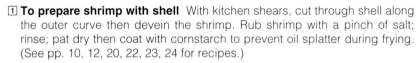

1. *Para preparar camarones con cáscara* Con tijeras de cocina, corte la cáscara por la curva exterior y desvene el camarón. Frote el camarón con una pizca de sal; enjuague; seque ligeramente y reboce con maicena para evitar que salpique el aceite cuando se fríe. (Vea pp. 10, 12, 20, 22, 23, 24 para recetas.)

2. *Para preparar camarones pelados* Pele los camarones. Haga un corte por la curva exterior para exponer la vena oscura; desvene. Frote 1/2 lb. (225g) de camarón con 1/2c. sal y 1 C. de agua, enjuague y escurra. (Vea pp. 11, 14-19, 21, 34, 35 para recetas.)

3. *Si el camarón es grande, córtelo por la mitad.*

4. *Sazone el camarón según la cantidad de camarones que usted use, después agregue la clara del huevo (opcional) y mezcle bien hasta que el agua se absorba completamente. Agregue maicena y mezcle bien. Agregue aceite mezclando para que los camarones se separen fácilmente cuando se fríen. Puede preparar los camarones y guardarlos en bolsas en el congelador para usarlos luego.*

Sugerencias para freír-revolviendo el camarón

5. *Si los ingredientes acompañados son demasiados secos cuando se fría-revolviendo, agregue 1 C. de agua. Fría-revolviendo y quite; tire el líquido.*

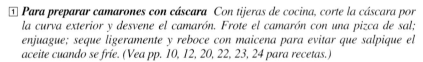

6. *Si el fuego no es suficientemente alto para freír-revolviendo, separe los camarones, sofría por 15 segundos, voltee los camarones, fría hasta que cambien de color por todos lados, luego regrese los ingredientes fritos y sazone.*

蟹的處理　Preparing Crab
Preparación de Cangrejo

1. 將活蟹用滾水沖燙取下蟹蓋，去鰓，並刷淨外殼。去除蟹蓋嘴上方之胃袋，蟹黃可食，蟹蓋可切塊或整塊使用。
2. 蟹身分切6或8塊，若蟹身大可將蟹腳切下，將蟹腳及鉗的硬殼鎚破，便於食用。
□ 煎或炸蟹塊前需拭乾水份，再洒太白粉，以免油爆。(蟹料理見 P. 62-68, 70, 71, 74)

1. Pour boiling water over the live crab; remove the shell and gills; scrub the shell clean. Remove the stomach located above its mouth under the shell, but save crab spawn. The crab shell can be cut into pieces or kept whole.
2. Cut the body of the crab into 6 or 8 pieces. Cut off the legs if the crab is big. Crack the shells of the claws and legs with a meat mallet for ease of eating.
□ To prevent oil splatter while frying, thoroughly pat the crab dry then coat with cornstarch before frying. (See pp. 62-68, 70, 71, 74 for recipes.)

1. *Vacíe agua hirviendo sobre el cangrejo vivo; quítele el carapacho y las entrañas; talle el carapacho hasta limpiarlo bien. Sáquele el estómago localizado arriba de la boca abajo del carapacho, pero guarde la hueva del cangrejo. El carapacho se puede cortar en pedazos o dejar entero.*
2. *Corte el cuerpo del cangrejo en 6 u 8 piezas. Si el cangrejo es grande quítele las piernas. Rompa la cáscara de las pinzas y las piernas con un machacador de carne para que sea más fácil de comer.*
□ *Para evitar que salpique el aceite mientras fríe, seque ligeramente todo el cangrejo luego rebócelo con maicena antes de freír. (Vea pp. 62-68, 70, 71, 74 para recetas.)*

魷魚或墨魚處理法　Preparing Squid or Cuttlefish
Preparación de Calamar o Jibia

3. 魷魚直切一刀打開來，去除軟骨內臟、眼及硬嘴，洗淨拭乾。
4. 魷魚片在內面輕劃一刀。
5. 翻面撕去外皮。
6. 在魷魚片內面斜劃刀，深至2/3處，轉一方向再斜劃刀成交叉紋。先切成寬條再切塊。(魷魚料理見76-85頁)

3. Cut the squid in half lengthwise; remove its long, transparent, sword-shaped shell, intestines, eyes, and beak; wash and pat dry.
4. Lightly slit the squid inside.
5. Turn it inside out; peel off the membrane. Prepared squid are available at the supermarket.
6. Make diagonal cuts to 2/3 deep on the inside surface; turn the squid and make diagonal cuts to 2/3 deep to form crisscross cuts. Cut them into wide strips then pieces. (See pp. 76-85 for recipes.)

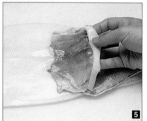

3. *Corte el calamar por la mitad a lo largo; quítele la larga y transparente concha en forma de espada, los intestinos, ojos y pico; lave y seque ligeramente.*
4. *Haga tajadas ligeras por dentro del calamar.*
5. *Voltéelo al revés; quítele la membrana. Puede comprar calamares ya preparados en el supermercado.*
6. *Haga cortes diagonales de 2/3 de profundidad en la superficie interior; voltee el calamar y haga tajadas diagonales de 2/3 de profundidad para formar tajadas en forma de equis. Córtelas en tiras anchas luego en pedazos. (Vea pp. 76-85 para recetas.)*

鹽水蝦

Camarones Salados

Salty Shrimp

蝦 ....半斤(300公克)

① 芥末粉 1大匙
水 2大匙

醬油 1大匙
水 4杯

② 酒 2大匙
鹽 2小匙
蔥 2條
薑 2大片

🦐 🦐 🦐

---

²/₃ lb. (300g) fresh shrimp

① 1 T. mustard powder
2 T. water

1 T. soy sauce
4 c. water

② 2 T. cooking wine
2 t. salt
2 green onions
2 slices ginger root

🦐 🦐 🦐

---

① 蝦處理乾淨(見8頁①)。將①料攪拌均勻用保鮮膜蓋緊，食時拌入醬油即成沾料；亦可用吃生魚片的沾料山葵醬取代。

② 水4杯加②料燒開，放入蝦煮至蝦變紅彎曲約2~3分鐘，蝦肉剛熟立即撈出置盤，趁熱沾沾料食用。

清蒸蝦 蝦拌入②料(鹽改成1/4小匙)，大火蒸4分鐘後再燜2分鐘，沾沾料食用。

🦐 🦐 🦐

---

²/₃ lb. (300g) camarones frescos

① *1 C. mostaza en polvo*
2 C. agua

1 C. salsa de soya
4 tz. agua

② *2 C. vino para cocinar*
2 c. sal
2 cebollines
2 rebanadas de raíz de jengibre

清蒸蝦・Steamed Shrimp
Camarones al Vapor

---

① Prepare shrimp (see p. 8, ①). Mix ① thoroughly in a bowl; cover tightly with plastic wrap. When serving, add soy sauce to ① to make the dip. Soy sauce may be substituted with Japanese horseradish paste, the dip used with raw fish.

② Bring 4 c. water along with ② to a boil; add shrimp; cook 2-3 minutes until red and curled. Remove immediately when done. Serve hot with the dip.

Steamed Shrimp Mix shrimp in ② (reduce salt to 1/4 t.). Steam shrimp over high heat for 4 minutes. Turn off the heat; cover and let steam for another 2 minutes; remove; serve with the dip.

🦐 🦐 🦐

① *Prepare los camarones (vea p. 8, ①). Mezcle ① completamente en un tazón; cubra bien con papel de plástico para envolver. Al servir, agregue salsa de soya a ① para hacer el dip. Puede substituir salsa de soya con pasta de rábano picante japonés para hacer el dip para pescado crudo.*

② *Hierva 4 tz. de agua con ②; agregue los camarones; cocine 2-3 minutos hasta que estén rojos y se enrosquen. Cuando estén listos saque inmediatamente. Sirva caliente con el dip.*

Camarones al Vapor *Mezcle los camarones en ②(reduzca la sal a 1/4 c.). Cocine los camarones al vapor sobre fuego alto por 4 minutos. Apague el fuego; cubra y siga cocinándolos por otros 2 minutos; saque; sirva con el dip.*

芝麻蝦球
Sesame Shrimp Balls
Bolas de Camarón con Sésamo

2人份・serves 2
2 porciones

大蝦仁 ....6兩(225公克)
小黃瓜(切片) 1杯
濕粉皮 * 1杯

①
芝麻醬或花生醬 1大匙
醬油 3大匙
醋、糖、辣豆瓣醬 各1/2大匙

②
蔥末 1大匙
蒜末 1/2大匙
麻油、辣油 各1/2大匙

∗∕ ∗∕ ∗∕

1/2 lb. (225g) large shelled
   shrimp
1 c. sliced gherkin
   cucumbers
1 c. fresh green bean
   starch sheet *

①
1 T. sesame paste or
   peanut butter
3 T. soy sauce
1/2 T. each: vinegar, sugar,
   chili bean paste

②
1 T. minced green onion
1/2 T. minced garlic cloves
1/2 T. each: sesame oil, chili
   oil

∗∕ ∗∕ ∗∕

1/2 lb. (225g) camarones grande sin
   cáscara
1 tz. de pepino gherkin en
   rebanadas
1 tz. hoja tiesa fresca de ejote *

①
1 C. pasta de sésamo o crema de
   cacahuate
3 C. salsa de soya
1/2 C. c/u: vinagre, azúcar, pasta
   de frijol picante

②
1 C. cebollín finamente picado
1/2 C. ajo finamente picado
1/2 C. c/u: aceite de sésamo,
   aceite de chile

∗∕ ∗∕ ∗∕

1

1 蝦仁處理乾淨（見8頁**2**），由背部輕劃二刀（圖1）。小黃瓜片泡冷水後瀝乾
置盤，濕粉皮用溫水略洗置其上。將 **①** 料仔細攪勻再加 **②** 料成沾料。

2 水4杯燒開，放入蝦煮至蝦變紅彎曲約2-3分鐘，蝦肉剛熟立即撈出置於粉皮
上，拌入沾料即成。

∗ 如用乾粉皮需放入滾水內泡30分鐘，瀝乾後切條，拌入油即可使用。

∗∕ ∗∕ ∗∕

1 Prepare the shrimp (see p. 8, **2**). Make 2 cuts lengthwise along the
outer curve of each shrimp (Fig. 1). Soak cucumber in cold water; drain
then arrange on a serving plate. Briefly rinse the bean starch sheet in warm
water and place on top of cucumber. Mix **①** thoroughly then add **②** to
make the dipping sauce.

2 Bring 4 c. water to boil; cook shrimp 2-3 minutes until red and curled;
remove instantly. Top bean sheet with shrimp; mix in sauce; serve.

∗ If dry green bean starch sheet is used, first soak in boiling water for
30 minutes; drain; cut into strips; mix in oil; ready for use.

∗∕ ∗∕ ∗∕

1 *Prepare los camarones (vea p. 8, **2**). Haga dos cortes a lo largo de la
curva exterior de cada camarón (Fig. 1). Remoje el pepino en agua fría;
cuele y arréglelos en el plato a servir. Brevemente enjuague la hoja de
ejote en agua tibia y coloque encima del pepino. Mezcle **①** completamente
y agregue **②** para hacer la salsa para dip.*

2 *Haga hervir 4 tz. de agua; cocine los camarones 2-3 minutos hasta que
estén rojos y se enrosquen; saque inmediatamente. Cubra la hoja de ejote
con camarones; mezcle en la salsa; sirva.*

∗ *Si usa hoja tiesa de ejote seca, remójela en agua hirviendo por 30
minutos; cuele; corte en tiras; mezcle en aceite; está lista para usarse.*

燒酒蝦

Prawns in Wine

Camarones en Vino

2人份 · serves 2
2 porciones

大草蝦 12條
　或大明蝦 ....半斤(300公克)

① 水 1杯
　鹽 ....¹/₄小匙
　枸杞(圖1)* ....¹/₂大匙
　當歸(圖1)* 2大片

　米酒 ....1 杯

🐚　🐚　🐚

12 prawns, ²/₃ lb. (300g)

1 c. water
① **¹/₄ t. salt**
¹/₂ T. lycium berries (dried boxphorn fruit)*(Fig. 1)
2 dang guei slices* (Fig. 1)

1 c. rice wine

🐚　🐚　🐚

12 camarones grandes, ²/₃ lb. (300g)

1 tz. agua
¹/₄ c. sal
① *¹/₂ C. baya de licio (fruta seca boxphorn)* (Fig. 1)*
*2 rebanadas de dang guei * (Fig. 1)*

1 tz. vino de arroz

① 蝦處理乾淨(見8頁①)，將 ① 料泡3小時備用。

② 酒放入 ① 料內燒開，改中火煮5分鐘，隨入蝦煮至蝦變紅彎曲約2-3分鐘，蝦肉剛熟即可食用。煮蝦的湯汁可用來當湯喝。

燒酒蟹 蟹處理乾淨(見9頁)切塊，其他材料、做法參考燒酒蝦。

★ 枸杞養眼，當歸有補血作用，放少量增加香味，放多會苦。

🐚　🐚　🐚

① Prepare prawns (see p. 8, ①); marinate in ① for 3 hours.

② Bring ① and cooking wine to boil. Reduce heat to medium; continue cooking 5 minutes. Add prawns to pot; cook until red and curled. Remove and serve. The cooking liquid may be served as a soup.

Crab in Wine Prepare the crab (see p. 9). Cut into pieces. Procedures and other ingredients are the same as "Prawns in Wine".

★ Boxphorn fruit is good for the eyes. Dang Guei nourishes and increases the blood supply. A small amount will enhance the flavor of the dish, but too much will create a bitter taste.

🐚　🐚　🐚

① *Prepare los camarones (vea p. 8, ①); marine en ① por 3 horas.*

② *Hierva ① y el vino para cocinar. Baje el fuego a moderado; continúe cocinando por 5 minutos. Agregue los camarones a la olla; cocine hasta que estén rojos y se enrosquen. Retire y sirva. El líquido se puede servir como sopa.*

Cangrejo en Vino Prepare el cangrejo (vea p. 9). Corte en pedazos. Los procedimientos y otros ingredientes son iguales que para "Camarones en Vino."

★ *La fruta boxphorn es buena para la vista. Dang Guei nutre y aumenta el abastecimiento de sangre. Una pequeña cantidad enriquecerá el sabor del platillo, pero mucha lo hará amargo.*

1

龍蝦沙拉

Lobster Salad

Ensalada de Langosta

龍蝦1隻 .... 1斤(600公克)
　　或蝦仁 .... 半斤(300公克)

① 馬鈴薯、紅蘿蔔(煮熟、切丁)..
　　................共12兩(450公克)
　 青豆仁(煮熟) 1/2杯

② 沙拉醬(美乃滋) 1/2杯
　 檸檬汁 ....數滴

🦐　🦐　🦐

1 lobster 1¹/₃ lbs. (600g) or
　²/₃ lb. (300g) shelled
　shrimp

① 1 lb. (450g) total, cooked
　and diced: potatoes,
　carrots
　¹/₂ c. cooked green peas

② ¹/₂ c. mayonnaise
　few drops of lemon juice

🦐　🦐　🦐

1 langosta 1¹/₃ lbs. (600g) o
　²/₃ lb. (300g) camarón pelado

① 1 lb. (450g) en total, cocido y
　picado: papas, zanahorias
　¹/₂ tz. chícharos cocidos

② ¹/₂ tz. mayonesa
　unas gotas de jugo de limón

宴客菜 · serve at formal meal
Se sirve en una comida formal

1. 龍蝦洗淨後由尾部插入一根筷子，以免蒸後龍蝦身彎曲。

2. 水燒開，大火將龍蝦蒸15分鐘至熟，取出筷子(圖1)及龍蝦頭(圖2)，龍蝦殼用剪刀剪開取出肉後切片，頭尾可用做裝飾。

3. 將龍蝦片、① 料及 ② 料拌勻，置於龍蝦殼的旁邊或頭與尾之間。① 料內的材料無限定，如鳳梨、蘋果等皆可使用。

🦐　🦐　🦐

1. Clean lobster. Thread a chopstick from the tail to the head of the lobster to prevent curling during steaming.

2. Bring water to a boil. Steam lobster over high heat until cooked through, about 15 minutes. Remove the chopsticks (Fig. 1) and head (Fig. 2). Cut through shell with kitchen shears to pull out the meat; slice and set aside. Reserve the lobster's head and tail to garnish the dish on a plate later.

3. Mix the lobster meat with ① and ② until combined. Arrange around the shell or between the head and the tail. Ingredients in ① are unlimited, i.e. pineapples, apples or other ingredients may be used.

🦐　🦐　🦐

1. *Limpie la langosta. Inserte un palillo chino de la cola a la cabeza de la langosta para prevenir que se enrosque cuando se esté cocinando a vapor.*

2. *Hierva el agua. Cocine la langosta a fuego alto hasta que esté cocida completamente, como por 15 minutos. Quítele el palillo (Fig. 1) y la cabeza (Fig. 2). Corte el carapacho con tijeras para cocina y sáquele la carne; rebane y deje aparte. Guarde la cabeza y la cola para adornar el platillo de servir.*

3. *Mezcle la carne de langosta con ① y ② completamente. Acomódela alrededor del carapacho o entre la cabeza y la cola. Los ingredientes en ① no son limitados, ej. piña, manzanas u otros ingredientes se pueden usar.*

1

2

玉米炒蝦仁　　　Shrimp & Corn

Camarones y Elote

蝦仁 ....6兩（225公克）

1 鹽 ....¹/₆小匙
酒、太白粉 各1大匙

2 蔥(3公分長) 8段
薑 4片

3 玉米粒 1杯
黃瓜(去籽、切丁) 1杯

4 水 .....4大匙，胡椒 .....¹/₈小匙
鹽、糖 ....各¹/₃小匙
太白粉、麻油 各1小匙

🦐　🦐　🦐

¹/₂ lb. (225g) shelled shrimp

1 ¹/₆ t. salt
1 T. each: cooking wine,
cornstarch

2 8 green onion sections, 1 ¹/₄"
(3cm) long
4 slices ginger root

3 1 c. corn kernels
1 c. cucumber, remove seeds
and dice

4 4 T. water, ¹/₈ t. pepper
¹/₃ t. each: salt, sugar
1 t. each: cornstarch, sesame
oil

🦐　🦐　🦐

¹/₂ lb. (225g) camarón pelado

1 ¹/₆ c. sal
1 C. c/u: vino para cocinar,
maicena

2 8 secciones de cebollines 1¹/₄"
(3cm) de largo
4 rebanadas de raíz de jengibre

3 1 tz. granos de elote
1 tz. pepino, quite las semillas
y pique

4 4 C. agua, ¹/₈ c. pimienta
¹/₃ c. c/u: sal, azúcar
1 c. c/u: maicena, aceite de
sésamo

1 蝦仁處理乾淨(見8頁**2**)，調入 **1** 料再拌油1大匙較容易炒開。

2 油1大匙燒熱，入 **3** 料略炒撈出。

3 油2大匙燒熱，炒香 **2** 料，入蝦仁炒開至變紅彎曲，再加炒好的 **3** 料及調勻的 **4** 料炒拌均勻即成。

蘆筍炒蝦仁 **3** 料改用蘆筍紅椒及毛菇，其他材料及做法如上。

🦐　🦐　🦐

1 Prepare shrimp (see p. 8, **2**)　Add **1** to the shrimp then 1 T. oil to separate shrimp easily during stir-frying.

2 Heat 1 T. oil. Stir in **3** briefly; remove.

3 Heat 2 T. oil. Stir-fry **2** until fragrant. Add shrimp to wok; continue stirring until shrimp are separated, red, and curled. Add **3** and mixture **4**; stir until combined; serve.

Shrimp & Asparagus Ingredients in **3** are substituted with asparagus, red pepper, and mushrooms. Other ingredients and steps remain the same as above.

🦐　🦐　🦐

1 *Prepare los camarones (vea p. 8, **2**). Agregue **1** a los camarones luego 1 C. de aceite para que se separen fácilmente mientras se fríen-revolviendo.*

2 *Caliente 1 C. de aceite. Agregue **3** brevemente; retire.*

3 *Caliente 2 C. de aceite. Fría-revolviendo **2** hasta que esté aromático. Agregue los camarones a la sartén wok; continúe revolviendo hasta que los camarones se separen, estén rojos y enroscados. Agregue **3** y mezcla **4**; revuelva hasta que se mezcle bien; sirva.*

Camarones y Espárragos *Los ingredientes del **3** se substituyen con espárragos, chile rojo y hongos. Los demás ingredientes y procedimientos son como los de arriba.*

蘆筍炒蝦仁・Shrimp & Asparagus
Camarones y Espárragos

花菜炒蝦仁

Shrimp & Broccoli

Camarones y Bróculi

蝦仁 ....6兩(225公克)
鹽 ....¹/₆小匙
酒、太白粉 各1大匙
蔥(3公分長) 8段
薑 4片

青花菜2杯 ....6兩(225公克)
水 3大匙
蠔油或醬油 1大匙
鹽、糖 ....各¹/₄小匙
胡椒 ....¹/₈小匙
太白粉、麻油 各1小匙

🐦 🐦 🐦

¹/₂ **lb. (225g) shelled shrimp**

¹/₆ **t. salt**
1 T. each: cooking wine,
  cornstarch

8 green onion sections,
  1¹/₄" (3cm) long
4 slices ginger root

2 c. broccoli, ¹/₂ lb. (225g)

3 T. water
1 T. oyster sauce or soy
  sauce
¹/₄ **t. each: salt, sugar**
¹/₈ **t. pepper**
1 t. each: cornstarch,
  sesame oil

🐦 🐦 🐦

¹/₂ *lb. (225g) camarones pelados*

¹/₆ *c. sal*
1 C. c/u: vino para cocinar,
  maicena

8 secciones de cebollines, 1¹/₄"
  (3cm) de largo
4 rebanadas de raíz de jengibre

2 tz. bróculi, ¹/₂ lb. (225g)

3 C. agua
1 C. salsa de ostión o salsa de
  soya
¹/₄ *c. c/u: sal, azúcar*
¹/₈ *c. pimienta*
1 c. c/u: maicena, aceite de
  sésamo

1

1 蝦仁處理乾淨(見8頁**2**)，調入 **1** 料再拌油1大匙較容易炒開。青花菜的花部切小朵，莖部削去皮(圖1)作其它用途。

2 油1大匙燒熱，入青花菜及水4大匙蓋鍋煮約2分鐘撈出，圍邊。

3 油2大匙燒熱，炒香 **2** 料，入蝦仁炒開至變紅彎曲，再加調勻的 **3** 料炒拌均勻置於有青花菜的盤中。

🐦 🐦 🐦

1 Prepare shrimp (see p. 8,**2**). Mix shrimp with **1** then with 1 T. oil to separate the shrimp easily during stir-frying. Cut broccoli head into small flowerets. Peel stems (Fig. 1) for other uses.

2 Heat 1 T. oil. Stir in broccoli and 4 T. water. Cover and cook about 2 minutes; remove. Arrange broccoli around the edge of a serving plate.

3 Heat 2 T. oil. Stir-fry **2** until fragrant. Add shrimp; stir-fry until shrimp are red, curled, and separated. Then add mixture **3** to wok, mix well and spatula into the center of the serving plate inside the broccoli circle. Serve.

🐦 🐦 🐦

1 *Prepare los camarones (vea p. 8, **2**). Mezcle los camarones con **1** luego con 1 C. de aceite para que se separen fácilmente cuando se fría-revolviendo. Corte las cabezas del bróculi en florecitas. Pele tallos (Fig. 1) para otros usos.*

2 *Caliente 1 C. de aceite. Agregue revolviendo el bróculi y 4 C. de agua. Tape y cocine por 2 minutos; retire. Acomode el bróculi alrededor de la orilla del plato de servir.*

3 *Caliente 2 C. de aceite. Fría-revolviendo **2** hasta que esté aromático. Agregue los camarones; fría-revolviendo hasta que los camarones estén rojos, se enrosquen, y se separen. Luego agregue la mezcla **3** a la sartén wok, mezcle bien y con una espátula agregue la mezcla al centro del plato de servir adentro del círculo de bróculi. Sirva.*

宮保炒蝦仁　Shrimp & Chili Pepper

Camarones con Chile

2人份・serves 2
2 porciones

蝦仁 ....8兩(300公克)

① 鹽 1/6小匙
　 酒、太白粉 各1大匙

② 乾辣椒(切段去籽、圖1) 3條
　 蔥(3公分長) 10段

③ 水、醬油 各2大匙
　 糖 2小匙
　 醋、太白粉、麻油 各1小匙

炸腰果或花生 1/2杯

🌿　🌿　🌿

²/₃ lb. (300g) shelled shrimp

① **1/6 t. salt**
　**1 T. each: cooking wine,
　cornstarch**

② **3 dried chili peppers, cut
　into pieces and seeds
　removed (Fig. 1)**
　**10 green onion sections,
　1¹/₄" (3cm) long**

③ **2 T. each: water, soy sauce**
　2 t. sugar
　**1 t. each: vinegar,
　cornstarch, sesame oil**

**¹/₂ c. cashews or peanuts,
fried**

🌿　🌿　🌿

**²/₃ lb. (300g) camarones
pelados**

① *1/6 c. sal*
　*1 C. c/u: vino para cocinar,
　maicena*

② *3 chiles secos, corte en pedazos
　y quíteles las semillas (Fig. 1)*
　*10 secciones de cebollines, 1¹/₄"
　(3cm) de largo*

③ *2 C. c/u: agua, salsa de soya*
　2 c. azúcar
　*1 c. c/u: vinagre, maicena,
　aceite de sésamo*

*¹/₂ tz. anacardos o cacahuates
dorados*

1 蝦仁處理乾淨(見8頁 **2**)，調入 ① 料再拌油1大匙較容易炒開。

2 油2大匙燒熱，炒香 ② 料，入蝦仁炒開至變紅彎曲，再加調勻的 ③ 料炒拌均勻，撒上腰果即成。

🌿　🌿　🌿

1 Prepare shrimp (see p. 8, **2**). Mix shrimp in ① then with 1 T. oil to separate shrimp easily during stir-frying.

2 Heat 2 T. oil. Stir-fry ② until fragrant. Add shrimp; stir-fry until shrimp are separated, red, and curled. Add mixture ③; stir until well mixed. Sprinkle with fried cashews or peanuts. Serve.

🌿　🌿　🌿

1 *Prepare los camarones (vea p. 8, **2**). Agregue mezclando los camarones a ① luego 1 C. de aceite para que se separen fácilmente cuando fría-revolviendo.*

2 *Caliente 2 C. de aceite. Fría revolviendo ② hasta que esté aromático. Agregue los camarones; fría-revolviendo hasta que los camarones se separen, estén rojos y enroscados. Agregue la mezcla ③ ; revuelva hasta que se mezcle bien. Coloque encima los anacardos o cacahuates. Sirva.*

1

豉汁炒蝦仁　　Shrimp & Bean Sauce
Camarones y Salsa de Frijol

蝦仁 ....半斤(300公克)

1
鹽 1/4小匙
酒、太白粉 各1 1/3大匙

2
豆豉*(略切) 1大匙
蒜、辣椒(切碎) 各1小匙
蔥(3公分長) 12段

3
水 ......3大匙，太白粉 1小匙
醬油 1/2大匙
糖、麻油 各1/2小匙

🥄　🥄　🥄

1
2/3 lb. (300g) shelled
　shrimp

1/4 t. salt
1 1/3 T. each: cooking wine,
cornstarch

2
1 T. fermented black
　beans*, cut in pieces
1 t. each: minced garlic
　cloves and chili pepper
12 green onion sections,
1 1/4" (3cm) long

3
3 T. water, 1 t. cornstarch
1/2 T. soy sauce
1/2 t. each: sugar, sesame
　oil

🥄　🥄　🥄

1
2/3 lb. (300g) camarones
　pelados

1/4 c. sal
1 1/3 C. c/u: vino para cocinar,
maicena

2
1 C. frijoles negros
　fermentados*, cortados en
　pedazos
1 c. c/u: ajo finamente picado y
　chile
12 secciones de cebollines, 1 1/4"
(3cm) de largo

3
3 C. agua, 1 c. maicena
1/2 C. salsa de soya
1/2 c. c/u: azúcar, aceite de
　sésamo

1

1 蝦仁處理乾淨(見8頁 **2**)，調入 **1** 料再拌油1大匙較容易炒開。

2 油3大匙燒熱炒香 **2** 料，入蝦仁炒開至變紅彎曲，再加調勻的 **3** 料炒拌均勻即成。

★ 豆豉(圖1)是烏豆蒸熟經發酵加鹽水釀製，有乾與濕，其用途相同。

🥄　🥄　🥄

1 Prepare shrimp (see p. 8, **2**). Mix shrimp with **1** then with 1 T. oil to separate shrimp easily during stir-frying.

2 Heat 3 T. oil. Stir-fry **2** until fragrant. Add shrimp; stir-fry until shrimp are red and curled. Add mixture **3** ; stir until well mixed. Serve.

★ Fermented black beans (Fig. 1) are cooked beans that have been marinated in salty water. Either dry or wet black beans can be used for cooking.

🥄　🥄　🥄

1 *Prepare los camarones (vea p. 8, **2**). Mezcle los camarones con **1** luego con 1 C. de aceite para que los camarones se separen fácilmente mientras se fríen revolviendo.*

2 *Caliente 3 C. de aceite. Fría-revolviendo **2** hasta que esté aromático. Agregue los camarones; fría-revolviendo hasta que los camarones estén rojos y enroscados. Agregue la mezcla **3** ; revuelva hasta que esté bien mezclado. Sirva.*

★ *Frijoles negros fermentados (Fig. 1) son frijoles cocidos que se escabecharon en agua salada. Puede usar frijoles negros remojados o secos para cocinar.*

滑蛋蝦仁　　Shrimp & Sleek Eggs

Camarones y Huevos Brillantes

2人份・serves 2
2 porciones

蝦仁 ....4兩(150公克)

① 鹽 1/8小匙
酒、太白粉 各2/3大匙

② 洋菇(新鮮或罐頭) 1/3杯
青豆仁或蔥花 1/3杯

③ 蛋 5個
鹽、糖 各1/3小匙
胡椒 1/8小匙

🦐　🦐　🦐

1/3 lb. (150g) shelled shrimp

① 1/8 t. salt
2/3 T. each: cooking wine, cornstarch

② 1/3 c. fresh or canned button mushrooms
1/3 c. green peas or chopped green onions

③ 5 eggs, beaten
1/3 t. each: salt, sugar
1/8 t. pepper

🦐　🦐　🦐

1/3 lb. (150g) camarones pelados

① 1/8 c. sal
2/3 C. c/u: vino para cocinar, maicena

② 1/3 tz. hongos frescos o enlatados
1/3 tz. chícharos o cebollines picados

③ 5 huevos, bien batidos
1/3 c. c/u: sal, azúcar
1/8 c. pimienta

1 蝦仁處理乾淨(見8頁 **2**)，調入 **1** 料再拌油1大匙(圖1)較容易炒開。

2 油2大匙燒熱，入蝦仁炒開至變紅彎曲，隨入 **2** 料略炒，再入打散的 **3** 料(油不夠時可酌量加入)用鍋鏟輕炒拌至蛋汁略凝固即成。

□ 此菜餚要炒得滑嫩，蛋汁略凝固時需立即起鍋。

🦐　🦐　🦐

1 Prepare shrimp (see p. 8, **2**). Mix shrimp with **1** then with 1 T. oil to separate shrimp easily during stir-frying (Fig. 1).

2 Heat 2 T. oil. Add shrimp; stir-fry until red and curled. Stir in **2** lightly; add mixture **3** (add more oil if needed); stir lightly until eggs are slightly set. Remove and serve.

□ The specialty of this dish is in the smoothness of the eggs. To make the dish successfully, remove eggs immediately when slightly set.

🦐　🦐　🦐

1 *Prepare los camarones (vea p. 8, **2**). Mezcle los camarones con **1** luego con 1 C. de aceite para que los camarones se separen fácilmente mientras se fríen revolviendo (Fig. 1).*

2 *Caliente 2 C. de aceite. Agregue los camarones; fría-revolviendo hasta que estén rojos y enroscados. Agregue mezclando **2** ligeramente; agregue la mezcla **3** (agregue más aceite si lo necesita); mezcle ligeramente hasta que los huevos estén un poco cuajados. Retire y sirva.*

□ *La especialidad de este platillo está en la suavidad de los huevos batidos. Para preparar este platillo exitosamente, retire los huevos inmediatamente cuando estén un poco cuajados.*

1

蝦仁豆腐 Shrimp & Bean Curd

Camarones con Tofu

蝦仁 ....4兩(150公克)

鹽 1/8小匙
酒、太白粉 各2/3大匙

蔥花 1大匙
薑 4片

番茄(切丁) ....6兩(225公克)
洋菇(切丁)、青豆仁 各1/3杯

豆腐(切丁) ....6兩(225公克)

高湯或水 1杯
醬油 ....1大匙，胡椒......1/8小匙
鹽、糖、麻油 各3/4小匙
太白粉 1大匙

❧ ❧ ❧

1/3 lb. (150g) shelled shrimp

1/8 t. salt
**2/3 T. each: cooking wine,
    cornstarch**

1 T. chopped green onions
4 slices ginger root

1/2 lb. (225g) diced tomato
**1/3 c. each: diced
    mushrooms, green peas**

**1/2 lb. (225g) bean curd
    chunks, 1" (2.5cm) square**

1 c. stock or water
1 T. soy sauce, 1/8 t. pepper
**3/4 t. each: salt, sugar,
    sesame oil**
1 T. cornstarch

❧ ❧ ❧

1/3 lb. (150g) camarones pelados

1/8 c. sal
*2/3 C. c/u: vino para cocinar,
    maicena*

1 C. cebollín picado
4 rebanadas de raíz de jengibre

1/2 lb. (225g) tomate picado
*1/3 tz. c/u: hongos picados,
    chícharos*

*1/2 lb. (225g) pedazos de tofu,
    cuadros de 1" (2.5cm)*

1 tz. caldo o agua
1 C. salsa de soya, 1/8 c. pimienta
*3/4 c. c/u: sal, azúcar, aceite de
    sésamo*
1 C. maicena

1 蝦仁處理乾淨(見8頁**2**)，調入 ❶ 料再拌油1大匙較容易炒開。

2 油2大匙燒熱，炒香 ❷ 料，入蝦仁炒開至變紅彎曲，隨入 ❸ 料略炒，再加豆腐及調勻的 ❹ 料炒拌至濃稠狀即成。

□ 若是蝦仁太大，可片開二(圖1)中間再劃一刀。

❧ ❧ ❧

1 Prepare shrimp (see p. 8, **2**). Mix shrimp with ❶ and 1 T. oil to separate the shrimp easily during stir-frying.

2 Heat 2 T. oil. Stir-fry ❷ until fragrant. Add shrimp; stir-fry until red and curled. Stir in ❸ lightly; add bean curd chunks and mixture ❹ ; cook until thickened. Remove and serve.

□ If large shrimp are used, slice in half lengthwise (Fig. 1) then make a slit along each half.

❧ ❧ ❧

1 *Prepare los camarones (vea p. 8, **2**). Mezcle los camarones con ❶ y 1 C. de aceite para que los camarones se separen fácilmente mientras se fríen-revolviendo.*

2 *Caliente 2 C. de aceite. Fría-revolviendo ❷ hasta que esté aromático. Agregue los camarones; fría-revolviendo hasta que estén rojos y enroscados. Agregue mezclando ❸ ligeramente; agréguele los pedazos de tofu y la mezcla ❹ ; cocine hasta que espese. Retire y sirva.*

□ *Si usa camarones grandes, rebánelos por la mitad a lo largo (Fig. 1) luego hágale un corte a cada mitad.*

1

乾煎蝦
Fried Shrimp

Camarones Sofritos

無頭蝦12條 ......半斤(300公克)

①
鹽 ....¹/₄小匙
酒、太白粉 ....各¹/₂大匙

②
蛋黃 2個
水 ....¹/₂大匙
麵粉 1¹/₄大匙

③
香菜末 1大匙
火腿末 1大匙

🐚　　🐚　　🐚

**12 beheaded prawns, ²/₃ lb.
(300g)**

①
¹/₄ t. salt
¹/₂ T. each: cooking wine,
   cornstarch

②
2 egg yolks
¹/₂ T. water
1¹/₄ T. flour

③
1 T. minced coriander
1 T. minced ham

🐚　　🐚　　🐚

*12 camarones grandes sin
   cabeza, ²/₃ lb. (300g)*

①
¹/₄ c. sal
*¹/₂ C. c/u: vino para cocinar,
   maicena*

②
2 yemas de huevo
¹/₂ C. agua
1¹/₄ C. harina

③
1 C. cilantro finamente picado
1 C. jamón finamente picado

1 蝦連殼由背部切開腹部仍相連，挑去腸泥，洗淨拭乾後在蝦肉面輕劃刀(使易入味，煎時不變形)，再拌入 **①** 料備用。

2 將蝦肉面朝上，抹上調勻的 **②** 料再以 **③** 料點綴(圖1)。

3 油2大匙燒熱，蝦殼朝下以中火煎(圖2)至蝦殼變色，蓋鍋燜至肉熟(前後共約3分鐘)即成。

🐚　　🐚　　🐚

1 Make a cut at the outer curve of each shelled shrimp to butterfly. Devein the shrimp; wash and pat dry. Score the inside surface lightly to absorb sauces easily and to prevent curling during frying. Marinate in **①**; set aside.

2 Spread mixture **②** on shrimp, meat side up. Garnish with **③** (Fig. 1).

3 Heat 2 T. oil. Pan-fry the shrimp, shells side down (Fig. 2), over medium heat until shrimp change color; cover and cook until cooked through, about 3 minutes total. Remove and serve.

🐚　　🐚　　🐚

1 *Haga una tajada en la curva exterior de cada camarón pelado para abrirlos. Desvene los camarones y seque ligeramente. Haga unas cortaditas adentro de la superficie para absorber la salsa fácilmente y para que no se enrosquen al freír. Marine en **①**; deje aparte.*

2 *Unte la mezcla **②** sobre los camarones, la carne boca arriba. Adorne con **③** (Fig. 1).*

3 *Caliente 2 C. de aceite. Sofría los camarones, cáscara abajo (Fig. 2) a fuego moderado hasta que los camarones cambien de color; cubra y cocine hasta que estén cocidos completamente, unos 3 minutos en total. Retire y sirva.*

1

2

鳳尾蝦　　　Phoenix Tail Prawns
Camarones Fénix con Cola

無頭蝦12條 ......4兩（150公克）

鹽 ....¹/₆小匙	
酒、太白粉 ....各¹/₂大匙	
土司麵包 6片	
蛋白 4個	
麵粉 3大匙	
太白粉 1大匙	
火腿末 1小匙	
黑芝麻 1小匙	
香菜 24片	
「炸油」 ....適量	

12 beheaded prawns,¹/₃ lb. (150g)

¹/₆ t. salt
¹/₂ T. each: cooking wine, cornstarch

6 bread slices
4 egg whites

3 T. flour
1 T. cornstarch

1 t. minced ham
1 t. black sesame seeds
24 coriander leaves

oil for deep-frying

12 camarones grandes sin cabeza, ¹/₃ lb. (150g)

¹/₆ c. sal
¹/₂ C. c/u: vino para cocinar, maicena

6 rebanadas de pan
4 claras de huevo

3 C. harina
1 C. maicena

1 c. jamón finamente picado
1 c. semillas de sésamo negras
24 hojas de cilantro

aceite para freír

1 蝦去殼留尾洗淨由背切開，腹部相連成一大片，拌入 **1** 料略醃。麵包去硬邊再切半。蛋白用打蛋器打至起白泡約8分鐘，加入 **2** 料拌勻即成蛋糊。

2 每片麵包上塗少許蛋糊，放上蝦(切開面朝下)，再把蛋糊蓋滿，四周抹平，上面以 **3** 料點綴。

3 「炸油」燒熱，蝦面朝下，以中小火炸約6分鐘(起鍋前需改大火炸)即成。

1 Shell the prawns but leave tails intact. Clean and make a cut along the outer curve of each prawn to butterfly; devein. Marinate the prawns in **1** briefly. Cut off the crusts from the slices of bread; halve each slice. To form a batter: Beat egg whites until frothy, about 8 minutes; stir in **2**, until blended.

2 Spread batter on each slice of bread; place the prawns (cut side down) on each slice of bread. Spread the remaining batter evenly over the prawns and the bread. Garnish with **3**.

3 Heat oil for deep-frying. Fry the prawns, cut side down, over medium low heat for 6 minutes. Increase heat to high just before ending the cooking. Remove and serve.

1 *Pele los camarones dejando la cola intacta. Limpie y haga un corte en la curva exterior de cada camarón para abrirlos; desvene. Marine los camarones brevemente en* **1**. *Quítele la corteza al pan; corte cada rebanada por la mitad. Para preparar la mezcla: Bata las claras de huevo hasta que se pongan espumosas, por unos 8 minutos; agregue revolviendo* **2**, *hasta que esté bien mezclado.*

2 *Unte el batido en ambos lados del pan; Coloque los camarones (corte abajo) sobre cada rebanada de pan. Unte la mezcla restante por partes iguales sobre los camarones y el pan. Adorne con* **3**.

3 *Caliente suficiente aceite para freír. Fría los camarones, corte abajo, sobre fuego moderado por 6 minutos. Aumente el fuego hasta alto inmediatamente antes que se acaben de cocinar. Retire y sirva.*

紫菜蝦腿　　　　　　　　Shrimp in Nori

Camarones en Nori

無頭蝦20條 ....6兩(225公克)

① 酒 1/2大匙
　　鹽 1/6小匙

② 蝦仁 ....6兩(225公克)
　　蔥 2枝
　　荸薺或洋蔥 1/3杯

③ 鹽 1/4小匙
　　糖、太白粉 各1小匙
　　麻油 1/8小匙

　　紫菜(20公分×20公分) 5張

④ 麵粉 ......3大匙，水 4大匙

　　「炸油」 ....適量

🦐　🦐　🦐

20 beheaded shrimp, 1/2 lb. (225g)

① **1/2 T. cooking wine**
1/6 t. salt

② **1/2 lb. (225g) shelled shrimp**
2 green onions
1/3 c. water chestnuts or onions

③ **1/4 t. salt**
1 t. each: sugar, cornstarch
1/8 t. sesame oil

5 nori sheets, 8"x 8" (20cm x 20cm)

④ **3 T. flour, 4 T. water**

oil for deep-frying

🦐　🦐　🦐

20 camarones sin cabeza, 1/2 lb. (225g)

① *1/2 C. vino para cocinar*
1/6 c. sal

② *1/2 lb. (225g) camarones pelados*
2 cebollines
1/3 tz. castañas de agua o cebolla

③ *1/4 c. sal*
1 c. c/u: azúcar, maicena
1/8 c. aceite de sésamo

5 hojas de nori, 8" x 8" (20cm x 20cm)

④ *3 C. harina, 4 C. agua*

aceite para freír

1

1 蝦去殼僅留尾(圖1)，抽出腸泥洗淨拭乾水份拌入 ❶ 料備用。

2 將 ❷ 料剁碎加 ❸ 料調勻，分成20份餡。紫菜每張切四，❹ 料調成麵糊。

3 紫菜四邊塗上麵糊，餡置中央，蝦置上露出蝦尾包成三角形。

4 「炸油」燒至八分熱350°F(180°C)，入蝦炸約3分鐘撈出，沾椒鹽或番茄醬食用。

🦐　🦐　🦐

1 Shell the shrimp but leave tails intact (Fig. 1). Devein the shrimp; rinse, and pat dry. Marinate the shrimp in ❶ ; set aside.

2 Chop ❷ and mix it with ❸ for the filling. Divide filling into 20 portions. Cut each nori in quarters. Stir ❹ into a paste.

3 Spread paste on the edges of each nori. Place a portion of the filling in the nori center. Put a shrimp over the filling, leave the tail outside the nori. Fold the nori to cover the shrimp; leave the tail unwrapped. Follow same procedures to make 19 more.

4 Heat oil for deep-frying to medium high, 350°F (180°C). Deep-fry the shrimp for about 3 minutes; remove. Serve Szechuan peppercorn salt or ketchup as a dip with shrimp.

🦐　🦐　🦐

1 *Pele los camarones dejando la cola intacta (Fig. 1). Desvene los camarones; enjuague, y seque ligeramente. Marine los camarones en ❶ ; deje aparte.*

2 *Corte en pedazos ❷ y mezcle con ❸ para el relleno. Divida el relleno en 20 porciones. Corte cada nori en cuartos. Bata ❹ formando una pasta.*

3 *Unte la pasta en las orillas de cada nori. Coloque una porción del relleno en el centro del nori. Ponga un camarón sobre el relleno, deje la cola afuera del nori. Doble el nori para cubrir el camarón; no envuelva la cola. Siga el mismo procedimiento para hacer 19 más.*

4 *Caliente aceite para freír-revolviendo a fuego alto moderado, 350°F (180°C). Fría revolviendo los camarones por unos 3 minutos; retire. Sirva los camarones con sal de grano de pimienta Szechuan o salsa de catsup para dip.*

Shrimp & Vegetables

Camarones y Vegetales

4人份・serves 4
4 porciones

無頭蝦20條 ....6兩（225公克）

1 酒 1/2大匙
鹽 1/6小匙

2 鹽 ....1/2小匙，糖 2小匙
蛋 ....1個，水 3/4杯

3 青椒、紅蘿蔔、香菇、蔥 ....
...................................切碎共11/2杯

麵粉 1杯
「炸油」 ....適量

ৡ৯   ৡ৯   ৡ৯

**20 beheaded shrimp, 1/2 lb.
(225g)**

1 **1/2 T. cooking wine**
1/6 t. salt

2 **1/2 t. salt, 2 t. sugar**
1 egg, 3/4 c. water

3 **11/2 c. total, minced:**
green pepper, carrot,
Chinese black mushrooms,
green onions

1 c. flour
oil for deep-frying

ৡ৯   ৡ৯   ৡ৯

*20 camarones sin cabeza, 1/2 lb.
(225g)*

1 *1/2 C. vino para cocinar*
1/6 c. sal

2 *1/2 c. sal, 2 c. azúcar*
1 huevo, 3/4 tz. agua

3 *11/2 tz. en total, finamente*
picado: pimiento, zanahoria,
hongos negros chinos, cebollín

1 tz. harina
aceite para freír

1 蝦去殼僅留尾，抽出腸泥洗淨拭乾，拌入 **1** 料備用。

2 將 **2** 料拌勻，再加麵粉及 **3** 料攪成麵糊(圖1)。

3 「炸油」燒至八分熱350°F(180°C)，將蝦沾裹麵糊(圖2)炸約4分鐘(剛入材料時油溫會下降，可用大火等溫度回升再以中火炸)呈金黃色撈出，沾椒鹽或番茄醬食用。

ৡ৯   ৡ৯   ৡ৯

1 Shell the shrimp but leave tails intact. Devein the shrimp; clean, and pat dry. Mix the shrimp in **1**. Set aside.

2 Mix **2** thoroughly; add flour and **3** to form a flour batter (Fig. 1).

3 Heat oil for deep-frying to medium high, 350°F (180°C); coat the shrimp with flour batter (Fig. 2) then fry 4 minutes until golden brown. For best results, maintain deep-frying oil at 350°F (180°C). When shrimp first contact the oil, the oil temperature drops. Increase heat to high until it reaches 350°F (180°C). Reduce heat to medium and continue frying process. Remove shrimp and serve with Szechuan peppercorn salt or ketchup as a dip.

ৡ৯   ৡ৯   ৡ৯

1 *Pele los camarones dejando la cola intacta. Desvene los camarones limpie y séquelos. Mézclelos en **1**. Deje aparte.*

2 *Mezcle **2** completamente; agregue harina y **3** para hacer el batido de harina (Fig. 1).*

3 *Caliente bastante aceite para freír a fuego alto; 350ºF (180ºC); reboce los camarones con el batido de harina (Fig. 2) luego fría por 4 minutos hasta que estén dorados. Para mejores resultados, mantenga el aceite para freír a 350ºF (180ºC). Cuando se sumergen los camarones en el aceite, la temperatura del aceite baja. Aumente el fuego a alto hasta que regrese a 350ºF (180ºC). Baje el fuego a alto moderado para continuar friendo. Retire los camarones y sirva con sal de grano de pimienta Szechuan o catsup como dip.*

1

2

蛋黃大蝦
Prawn Egg Rolls

大蝦 6條

① 酒 1小匙
鹽、胡椒 ....各 1/8小匙

太白粉 1杯

② 蛋 1個
太白粉 4大匙

生鹹蛋黃 6個
紫菜(3公分×6公分) 6張
「炸油」 ....適量

🐌   🐌   🐌

6 prawns

① 1 t. cooking wine
1/8 t. each: salt, pepper

1 c. cornstarch

② 1 egg
4 T. cornstarch

6 salty egg yolks
6 pieces nori, 1¼" x 2½"
  (3cm x 6cm)
oil for deep-frying

① 蝦去殼僅留尾，抽出腸泥洗淨拭乾，由背部切開成一大片，加 ① 料略醃，撒上太白粉後搥扁(圖1)。② 料拌勻。紫菜捲上蛋黃備用。

② 盤上備太白粉，蝦沾拌勻的 ② 料平鋪在粉上(蝦切口朝上)，將紫菜捲置蝦上(圖2)，捲成圓筒狀後沾滿太白粉備用。

③ 「炸油」燒至八分熱350°F(180℃)，入蝦捲炸約5分鐘(剛入材料時油溫會下降，可先用大火，油溫上升後再以中火炸)至金黃色皮酥肉熟撈出，切半置盤；這是一道精緻的宴客佳餚。

🐌   🐌   🐌

① Shell the prawns but leave tails intact. Devein prawns; rinse and pat dry. Cut lengthwise at the outer curve of each prawn to open it. Marinate the prawns in ① briefly. Sprinkle them with cornstarch; then flatten with a meat mallet (Fig. 1). Mix ② well. Put a salty egg yolk on a nori; roll it up; set aside.

② Place the prawns dipped in ② , cut side up, on a cornstarched plate. Place each nori roll on top of a prawn (Fig. 2), roll it to a cylinder; coat with cornstarch; set aside.

③ Heat oil for deep-frying to medium high, 350°F (180°C). Deep-fry the prawn rolls for 5 minutes or until golden brown and crispy. When prawn rolls first contact the oil, the oil temperature drops. Increase heat to high to bring the oil temperature back to 350°F (180°C); reduce heat to medium high; continue frying process. Remove prawns then cut each in half; place on a plate; serve.

1

2

Rollos de Camarones

Fotos a la izq.

Se sirve en una comida formal

camarones grandes
c. vino para cocinar
/8 c. c/u: sal, pimienta

tz. maicena

huevo
C. maicena

yemas de huevo saladas
pedazos de nori, 1¹/₄ " x 2¹/₂
  (3cm x 6cm)
ceite para freír

1 *Pele los camarones dejando la cola intacta. Desvene los camarones; enjuague y seque ligeramente. Corte la curva exterior a lo largo de cada camarón abriéndolos. Marine los camarones en* **1** *brevemente. Espolvoréelos con maicena; luego aplástelos con un machacador (p. 30, Fig. 1). Mezcle* **2** *completamente. Coloque una yema salada de huevo sobre cada nori; enrolle; deje aparte.*

2 *Coloque los camarones sumergidos en* **2** *, con la cortada arriba sobre un plato cubierto con maicena. Coloque cada nori arriba de los camarones (p. 30, Fig. 2), enrolle en forma de cilindro; reboce con maicena; deje aparte.*

3 *Caliente bastante aceite para freír a alto moderado, 350°F (180°C). Fría los rollos de camarones por 5 minutos o hasta que estén dorados y crujientes. Cuando se sumergen los rollos al aceite, la temperatura baja. Aumente el fuego a alto hasta que regrese a 350°F (180°C); baje el fuego a alto moderado; continúe el proceso de freír. Retírelos luego corte cada uno por la mitad; coloque en un plato; sirva.*

1

炸杏仁蝦片   Almond Shrimp

Camarones con Almendras

2人份 · Serves 2
2 porciones

1 蝦去殼僅留尾，抽出腸泥洗淨拭乾，由背部切開成一大片略搥扁(圖1)，拌入❶料，兩面沾裹杏仁片，用手略壓以防炸時脫落。

2 「炸油」燒熱，入蝦炸約2分鐘至金黃色肉熟，沾椒鹽或番茄醬食用。

🦐   🦐   🦐

1 Shell the shrimp but leave tails intact. Devein the shrimp; rinse and pat dry. Cut lengthwise at the outer curve of each shrimp to open, then flatten (Fig. 1). Mix shrimp in ❶ then coat with almonds; gently hand press almonds to prevent falling off during frying.

2 Heat oil for deep-frying; fry the shrimp 2 minutes or until golden brown and done. Remove and serve Szechuan peppercorn salt or ketchup as a dip for the shrimp.

🦐   🦐   🦐

大蝦 ....12兩(450公克)
酒 3/4大匙
鹽、胡椒 各1/6小匙
蛋白 1個
太白粉 1¹/₂大匙

杏仁片(或芝麻) 2杯
「炸油」.........................適量

🦐   🦐   🦐

lb. (450g) prawns or large
  shrimp
/4 T. cooking wine
/6 t. each: salt, pepper
  egg white
1¹/₂ T. cornstarch

c. almond slices or
  sesame seeds
il for deep-frying

🦐   🦐   🦐

lb. (450g) camarones grandes
  o medianos
/4 C. vino para cocinar
/6 c. c/u: sal, pimienta
  clara de huevo
¹/₂ C. maicena

tz. rebanadas de almendra o
  semilla de sésamo
ceite para freír

1 *Pele los camarones dejando la cola intacta. Desvene los camarones; enjuague y seque ligeramente. Corte la curva exterior a lo largo de cada camarón abriéndolos, luego aplástelos (Fig. 1). Mezcle los camarones en* ❶ *y cubra con las almendras; ligeramente aplane las almendras para que no se caigan al freír.*

2 *Caliente bastante aceite para freír; fría los camarones por 2 minutos o hasta que estén dorados y cocidos. Retire y sirva los camarones con sal de grano de pimienta Szechuan o catsup para dip.*

麵糊炸蝦
Deep-fried Shrimp

2人份 · serves 2

蝦 .... 12兩(450公克)

① 鹽 ....¹/₆小匙
酒、太白粉 ....各³/₄大匙

酥炸麵糊：

② 麵粉 1杯
發粉 ....¹/₂小匙

③ 水 ....³/₄杯
油 1大匙

軟乾麵糊：

④ 蛋 1個
冰水 ....⁴/₅杯
麵粉 ....1 杯

「炸油」 ....適量
椒鹽 ....適量

🍤　🍤　🍤

1 lb. (450g) shrimp

① ¹/₆ t. salt
³/₄ T. each: cooking wine,
cornstarch

Batter (crispy):

② 1 c. flour
¹/₂ t. baking powder

③ ³/₄ c. water
1 T. oil

Batter (soft):

④ 1 egg
⁴/₅ c. ice water
1 c. flour

oil for deep-frying
peppercorn salt as desired

1 蝦去殼僅留尾，抽出腸泥洗淨，拭乾水份，在腹部輕劃數刀(圖1)，以免炸時捲縮，調入 ❶ 料備用。將 ❷ 料混合，輕拌入 ❸ 料即成酥炸麵糊，或將 ❹ 料內的蛋打散再輕拌入冰水及麵粉即成軟炸麵糊。

2 「炸油」燒至八分熱350°F(180°C)，提起蝦尾沾裹酥炸或軟炸麵糊炸2-3分鐘，剛入材料時油溫會下降，可繼續以大火炸至金黃色外皮酥脆撈出，沾椒鹽食用。

麵糊魷魚、麵糊鮮貝 魷魚或鮮貝處理乾淨，其他材料做法如上。

🍤　🍤　🍤

1 Shell the shrimp but leave tails intact. Devein the shrimp, rinse and pat dry. Make several cuts on the inner curve (Fig. 1) to prevent curling during frying. Mix shrimp in ❶; set aside. Combine ❷ and ❸, stirring lightly to form a crispy batter. To form the soft batter, beat the egg in ❹; gently mix in ice water and flour; stir until just mixed.

2 Heat oil for deep-frying until oil reaches medium high, 350°F(180°C). Hold the shrimp by the tail; dip in the crispy or soft batter; deep-fry over high heat for 2-3 minutes or until golden and crispy. Remove. Serve Szechuan peppercorn salt or ketchup as a dip for the shrimp.

Deep-fried Squid, Deep-fried Scallops Clean the squid or scallops. Other ingredients and procedures are the same as above.

1

Camarones Fritos

Fotos a la izq.
2 porciones

1 lb. (450g) camarones
1/6 c. sal
1/4 C. c/u: vino para cocinar, maicena

Batido (crujiente):
1 tz. harina
1/2 c. polvo de hornear
3/4 tz. agua
1 C. aceite

Batido (suave):
1 huevo
1/5 tz. agua helada
1 tz. harina

aceite para freír
sal de grano de pimienta al gusto

1 Pele los camarones dejando la cola intacta. Desvene los camarones, enjuague y seque ligeramente. Haga varios cortes a la curva interior (p. 32, Fig. 1) para que no se enrosquen al freír. Mezcle los camarones en 1 ; deje aparte. Combine 2 y 3 , mezclando brevemente para formar un batido crujiente. Para hacer el batido suave, bata el huevo de 4 ; revuelva en cuanto esté poco mezclado.

2 Caliente bastante aceite para freír hasta que la temperatura llegue a alto moderado, 350°F (180°C). Tome el camarón por la cola; sumérjalo en el batido crujiente o suave; fría a fuego alto por 2-3 minutos o hasta que esté dorado y crujiente. Retire. Sírvalos con sal de grano de pimienta Szechuan o catsup como dip.

Calamar Frito, Escalopes Fritos Limpie el calamar o los escalopes. Los ingredientes y el procedimiento son iguales que los de esta receta.

糖醋炸蝦   Sweet & Sour Shrimp
Camarones Agridulces

2人份・Serves 2
2 porciones

酥炸蝦 ....6兩(225公克)
水 1/2杯
醬油、醋 各4大匙
檸檬汁 1大匙
糖 5大匙
辣椒醬(無亦可) 1/2小匙
太白粉 1大匙
麻油 1/2大匙

1 將酥炸蝦置盤(做法見左頁)。

2 將 1 料攪拌燒開成糊狀，淋在酥炸蝦上即成。

糖醋魷魚、糖醋鮮貝 將煮好的 1 料淋在酥炸魷魚或酥炸鮮貝上即成。

🦐 🦐 🦐

1/2 lb. (225g) deep-fried shrimp
1/2 c. water
4 T. each: soy sauce, vinegar
1 T. lemon juice
5 T. sugar
1/2 t. chili paste (optional)
1 T. cornstarch
1/2 T. sesame oil

1 Arrange crispy shrimp on a plate. (See left page for instructions to make deep-fried shrimp.)

2 Stir and bring 1 to a boil to form a liquid paste. Pour the paste over the crispy shrimp. Serve.

Sweat & Sour Squid, **Sweet & Sour Scallops** Pour the cooked 1 over the deep-fried squid or scallops; serve.

🦐 🦐 🦐

1/2 lb. (225g) camarones fritos
1/2 tz. agua
4 C. c/u: salsa de soya, vinagre
1 C. jugo de limón
5 C. azúcar
1/2 c. pasta de chile (opcional)
1 C. maicena
1/2 C. aceite de sésamo

1 Acomode los camarones crujientes sobre un plato. (Vea la página de arriba para preparar los camarones fritos.)

2 Mezcle y haga 1 hervir para hacer una pasta líquida. Vacíe la pasta sobre los camarones crujientes. Sirva.

Calamar Agridulce, Escalopes Agridulces Vacíe todo lo de 1 cocido sobre el calamar o los escalopes; sirva.

炸鑲蟹鉗
Crab Claws in Shrimp Balls 2人份・serves 2

冷凍蟹鉗 .... 半斤(300公克)
太白粉 1大匙
蝦仁 ....6兩(225公克)

①
鹽 1/4小匙
酒、太白粉 各1大匙
蛋白 1個

麵包粉 1/2杯
「炸油」 ....適量
椒鹽或番茄醬 ....適量

❧ ❧ ❧

²/₃ lb. (300g) frozen crab
  claws
1 T. cornstarch
¹/₂ lb. (225g) shelled
  shrimp

①
¹/₄ t. salt
1 T. each: cooking wine,
  cornstarch
1 egg white

¹/₂ c. bread crumbs
oil for deep-frying
peppercorn salt or ketchup
  as desired

1 蝦仁處理乾淨(見8頁**2**)，用機器攪碎或用鎚肉器搥成泥狀(愈細愈好)調入 **①** 料仔細拌勻成蝦漿。蟹鉗解凍後拭乾水份，蟹肉部份沾裹太白粉。

2 將蝦漿做成8個丸子，插入蟹鉗(圖1)沾裹麵包粉捏成橢圓形(圖2)。

3 「炸油」燒熱，入鑲好的蟹鉗炸約4分鐘(剛入材料時油溫會下降，可使用大火等溫度回升再以中火炸)呈金黃色略脹大即成，沾椒鹽或番茄醬食用。

❧ ❧ ❧

1 Prepare the shrimp (see p. 8, **2**). Whirl the shrimp in blender or smash the shrimp with a meat mallet until paste forms. The finer the shrimp grind, the better. Mix shrimp with **①** thoroughly to form the shrimp paste. Thaw and pat the claws dry. Coat the crab meat with cornstarch.

2 Form the shrimp paste into 8 balls. Insert a claw into each shrimp ball (Fig. 1). Roll the shrimp balls over bread crumbs, and shape into ovals (Fig. 2).

3 Heat oil for deep-frying; fry the shrimp balls with the claws 4 minutes or until golden and expanded a little. When the shrimp balls first contact the frying oil, the oil temperature drops. Increase the heat to high to bring the oil temperature back to 350°F (180°C), then lower heat to medium; continue frying process until done. Serve with Szechuan peppercorn salt or ketchup as a dip.

1

2

Pinzas de Cangrejo en Bolas de Camarón *Fotos a la izq.*

²/₃ lb. (300g) pinzas de cangrejo
   congeladas
1 C. maicena
¹/₂ lb. (225g) camarón pelado

¹/₄ c. sal
1 C. c/u: vino para cocinar,
   maicena
1 clara de huevo

¹/₂ tz. pan molido
aceite para freír
sal de grano de pimienta o
   catsup al gusto

1 Prepare los camarones (vea p. 8, **2**). Bata los camarones en una licuadora o macháquelos con un ablandador de carne hasta formar una pasta. Mientras más molidos estén los camarones, mejor. Mezcle los camarones con ❶ completamente para formar la pasta de camarón. Descongele y seque ligeramente las pinzas de cangrejo. Cubra la carne de cangrejo con maicena.

2 Forme la pasta de camarón en 8 bolas. Inserte una pinza de cangrejo a cada bola (p. 34, Fig. 1). Deslice las bolas de camarón sobre el pan molido y fórmelas en forma ovalada (p. 34, Fig. 2).

3 Caliente aceite para freír; fría las bolas de camarón con las pinzas de cangrejo por 4 minutos o hasta que estén doradas y se hayan expandido un poco. Cuando las bolas hacen contacto con el aceite, la temperatura del aceite baja. Suba el fuego a alto subiendo la temperatura del aceite de nuevo a 350°F (180°C), luego bájela a moderado; continúe el procedimiento hasta que termine de freír cada bola. Sirva con sal de grano de pimienta Szechuan o catsup como dip.

百角蝦丸　　Shrimp & Diced Bread

Bolas de Camarón

蝦仁 ....6兩(225公克)
❶ 料見左頁
凍麵包(隔夜的麵包)切丁 ...1杯
「炸油」 ....適量
椒鹽或番茄醬 ....適量

1 參照左頁作法 **1** 將蝦仁做成蝦漿，分做成8個丸子，滾上麵包丁備用。

2 「炸油」燒熱，入蝦丸炸約3分鐘即可(炸油溫度保持在350°F(180°C)左右炸出來的效果最好，溫度太低麵包易脫落，太高則易燒焦)。

℈   ℈   ℈

¹/₂ lb. (225g) shelled shrimp
❶ see left page
1 c. diced day old bread
oil for deep-frying
Szechuan peppercorn salt
   or ketchup as desired

1 Follow step **1** on the left page to make shrimp paste. Form the shrimp paste into 8 balls; roll the balls over the bread crumbs.

2 Heat oil for deep-frying. Fry shrimp balls about 3 minutes. For best results, maintain the frying oil temperature at 350°F (180°C). If the temperature is below that, the bread crumbs will easily fall off. If the temperature is above that, shrimp balls will quickly burn.

℈   ℈   ℈

¹/₂ lb. (225g) camarón pelado
❶ vea la receta de arriba
1 tz. pan seco en cubitos
aceite para freír
sal de grano de pimienta
   Szechuan o catsup al gusto

1 Siga el paso **1** de la receta de arriba para hacer la pasta de camarón. Forme la pasta en 8 bolas; deslice las bolas de camarón sobre el pan seco.

2 Caliente aceite para freír. Fría las bolas de camarón por 3 minutos. Para mejores resultados, mantenga el aceite a una temperatura de 350°F (180°C). Si la temperatura baja, el pan molido se caerá fácilmente. Si la temperatura es más alta, las bolas de camarón se quemarán rápidamente.

豉汁瓜子

Clams in Bean Sauce

2人份 · serves 2

海瓜子或其他貝類 ....
.........................12兩(450公克)

① 蔥、薑、蒜末 各1/2大匙
紅辣椒(切片) 1條

豆豉(切碎) 1大匙

② 水 3大匙
醬油 1/2大匙
糖、麻油 各1/2小匙
太白粉 1小匙

1 lb. (450g) live Manila
clams or other shellfish

① 1/2 T. each, minced: green
onion, ginger root, garlic
cloves
1 sliced red chili pepper

1 T. minced fermented black
beans

② 3 T. water
1/2 T. soy sauce
1/2 t. each: sugar, sesame
oil
1 t. cornstarch

1 海瓜子刷洗乾淨後瀝乾備用。

2 油2大匙燒熱，炒香 **①** 料及豆豉，隨入海瓜子及 **②** 料略炒(可蓋鍋)，將先開口的海瓜子逐一取出，全部開後，倒回炒拌均勻即可。

貝的選擇及處理　應選擇貝殼緊閉或貝殼略開一碰即閉的為新鮮；專賣店如是已浸在水內吐沙，買回來後只須將外殼刷洗乾淨即可用。否則宜用鹽水(水1杯、鹽1小匙的比例，圖1)水不必淹過貝，置數小時待吐沙後，刷洗表面才使用。如當天不用可暫置冰箱，使用當天再吐沙。

1 Scrub and wash clams, then drain.

2 Heat 2 T. oil. Stir-fry **①** and fermented black beans until fragrant. Add clams and **②**; stir-fry briefly. Remove the clams opened during cooking. Return the removed clams when all shells in the wok are open, mix well.

To prepare and select clams　Pick those fresh clams that are tightly closed or will close tightly when tapped. If clams purchased already have sand released in the store, scrub the clams clean, they are ready to use. If not, add salt to water at the ratio of 1 t. to 1 c. (Fig. 1). Soak clams in salty water several hours, water doesn't have to cover the clams. Scrub clams clean after the sand is released. Keep the clams in a refrigerator and soak to release sand the day when ready to use.

1

Almejas en Salsa de Frijol

lb. (450g) almejas Manila
   vivas u otro marisco

/2 C. c/u, finamente picado:
   cebollín, raíz de jengibre,
   diente de ajo
   chile rojo picado

C. frijoles negros fermentados,
   finamente machacados

C. agua
/2 C. salsa de soya
/2 c. c/u: azúcar, aceite de
   sésamo
c. maicena

1 Raspey lave las almejas, escurra.

2 Caliente 2 C. de aceite. Fría-revolviendo **1** y los frijoles hasta que esté aromático. Agregue las almejas y **2** ; fría-revolviendo brevemente. Saque las almejas que se abrieron durante la cocción. Regrese estas almejas a la sartén wok cuando todas las conchas en la sartén se hayan abierto, mezcle bien.

Para preparar y escoger almejas Escoja las almejas que tengan la concha bien cerrada o que se cierran con un golpe. Si las almejas que compra ya soltaron arena en la tienda, talle y lávelas bien, ya están listas para usar. Si no, agregue sal y agua proporcionado 1 c. a 1 tz. (p. 36, Fig. 1). Remoje las almejas en agua salada por varias horas, el agua no tiene que cubrir las almejas completamente. Talle y lávelas después que hayan soltado la arena. Mantenga las almejas en el refrigerador, remójelas para soltar la arena cuando vaya a usarlas.

酒烹海瓜子
Almejas en Vino
Clams in Wine

1 海瓜子刷洗乾淨後瀝乾備用。

2 油2大匙燒熱，炒香 **1** 料，隨入海瓜子及調勻的 **2** 料略炒(可蓋鍋)，將先開口的海瓜子逐一取出，全部開後倒回加九層塔炒拌均勻即成。

海瓜子或其他貝類 ....
..................12兩(450公克)
1 料同左

酒 1/3杯
鹽 1/4小匙
太白粉 1小匙

九層塔或香菜 1/2杯

🐚   🐚   🐚

1 lb. (450g) live Manila clams
   or other shellfish
the same as 1 of left page

1/3 c. cooking wine
1/4 t. salt
1 t. cornstarch

1/2 c. fresh basil or coriander

🐚   🐚   🐚

1 Scrub and wash clams; drain.

2 Heat 2 T. oil. Stir-fry **1** until fragrant; stir in clams and mixture **2** ; stir briefly. Remove the clams opened during cooking. Return the removed clams when all shells in the wok are open; add fresh basil; mix well. Serve.

🐚   🐚   🐚

1 lb. (450g) almejas Manila vivas u
   otro marisco
lo mismo que en 1 de la receta de
   arriba

1/3 tz. vino para cocinar
1/4 c. sal
1 c. maicena

1/2 tz. albahaca o cilantro fresco

1 Raspe y lave las almejas, escurra.

2 Caliente 2 C. de aceite. Fría-revolviendo **1** hasta que esté aromático; agregue revolviendo las almejas y la mezcla **2**, revuelva brevemente. Saque las almejas que se abrieron durante la cocción. Regrese estas almejas a la sartén wok cuando todas las conchas en la sartén se hayan abierto; agregue la albahaca fresca; mezcle bien. Sirva.

生炒貝肉
Stir-fried Clam Meat

貝類(任選) .... 1斤半(900公克)
豆苗或菠菜 ....6兩(225公克)

① 蔥(3公分長) 6段
　 薑 6片
　 紅辣椒(切片) 1條

② 洋菇、香菇、青菜 共2杯

③ 酒 1大匙
　 鹽、糖 各1/4小匙
　 胡椒、麻油 ....各少許
　 煮貝湯汁 4大匙
　 太白粉 1小匙

2 lbs. (900g) any clams
1/2 lb. (225g) snow pea
leaves or spinach

① 6 green onion sections, 11/4"
　　(3cm) long
　 6 slices ginger root
　 1 sliced red chili pepper

② 2 c. total: mushrooms and
　　vegetable leaves

③ 1 T. cooking wine
　 1/4 t. each: salt, sugar
　 pepper, sesame oil as
　　desired
　 4 T. liquid retained from
　　cooking shellfish
　 1 t. cornstarch

1 貝刷洗乾淨。水1杯燒開後倒入貝煮至殼微開即撈出取肉，湯汁留用。

2 油1大匙燒熱，入豆苗、鹽1/4小匙及水1大匙略炒，瀝乾水份置盤。

3 油2大匙燒熱，炒香 ① 料，隨入 ② 料略炒，再加貝肉及調勻的 ③ 料炒拌均勻盛在豆苗上，以貝殼圍邊。

蛤蜊清湯 滾水內放入哈唎、鹽煮至殼開，放入薑絲即成。

1 Scrub and wash clams. Pour 1 c. boiling water over clams. When opened, remove meat from shells. Reserve the cooking juice.

2 Heat 1 T. oil. Stir fry snow pea leaves, 1/4 t. salt, and 1 T. water briefly. Remove and discard cooking juice; transfer to a plate.

3 Heat 2 T. oil. Stir-fry ① until fragrant. Add ②; stir briefly; pour in clam meat and mixture ③; mix well. Remove; pour over snow pea leaves. Arrange shells around the shellfish meat.

Clam Soup Bring water to a boil. Add clams and salt to pot; cook until clams open. Sprinkle with shredded ginger. Remove and serve.

蛤蜊清湯 · Clam Soup
Sopa de Almeja

Carne de Almeja Semi-Frita

Fotos a la izq.

2 porciones

lbs. (900g) cualquier almeja
/2 lb. (225g) hojas de
    chícharos chinos o
    espinacas

secciones de cebollín, 1¼"
    (3cm) de largo

rebanadas de raíz de jengibre

chile rojo rebanado

tz. en total: hongos y hojas de
    vegetales

C. vino para cocinar

/4 c. c/u: sal, azúcar
    pimienta, aceite de sésamo
    al gusto

C. líquido restante del
    marisco cocido

c. maicena

1 *Raspe y lave las almejas. Vacíe 1 tz. de agua hirviendo sobre las almejas. Cuando se abran, sáquele la carne a las conchas. Guarde el caldo.*

2 *Caliente 1 C. de aceite. Fría-revolviendo las hojas de chícharos, 1/4 c. sal, y 1 C. agua brevemente. Retire y tire el caldo; ponga en un plato.*

3 *Caliente 2 C. de aceite. Fría-revolviendo* **1** *hasta que esté aromático. Agregue* **2** *revuelva brevemente; agregue la carne de almeja y la mezcla* **3***; mezcle bien. Retire; vacíe sobre las hojas de chícharos. Coloque las conchas alrededor de la carne.*

Sopa de Almeja *Ponga agua a hervir. Agregue las almejas y sal a la olla; cueza hasta que se abran las conchas. Espolvoree con jengibre rallado. Retire y sirva.*

烤蛤蜊

Almejas al Horno

Baked Clams

2人份 · serves 2
2 porciones

1 蛤蜊刷洗乾淨，每只蛤蜊之連接處用刀略剁斷或切去兩片韌帶(圖1、2)。此用意為使蛤蜊烤熟時不開口，湯汁就不易溢出。

2 將蛤蜊兩面沾水再沾鹽，烤箱燒熱至500°F(260°C)，入蛤蜊烤5分鐘不要烤過熟以免蛤蜊肉變硬。

෨ ෨ ෨

1 Scrub and wash clams. Cut off the joint of the shells with a knife or remove the 2 adductor muscles (Fig. 1 & Fig. 2) to prevent the shells from opening during baking.

2 Dip clams in water then salt on both shells. Bake 5 minutes in preheated 500°F (260°C) oven. Overbaking will make the meat tough.

෨ ෨ ෨

1 *Raspe y lave las almejas. Para prevenir que las conchas se abran durante la cocción, córtele la conjuntura a las conchas con un cuchillo o corte los 2 músculos aductores (Fig. 1 y Fig. 2).*

2 *Sumerja las almejas en agua después en sal por ambos lados. Hornee por 5 minutos en el horno precalentado a 500°F (260°C). El hornear demasiado hará que la carne no esté tierna.*

大蛤蜊 12個
鹽 ....適量

෨ ෨ ෨

12 large clams
salt as desired

෨ ෨ ෨

12 almejas grandes
sal al gusto

1

2

海瓜子燴麵線　Noodle Strings & Clams

Fideos y Almejas

海瓜子或其他貝類 ....
......................12兩(450公克)

(1) 薑、蒜末 各1大匙
辣椒(切碎) 1條

(2) 鹽、糖 各1/4小匙
麻油 1小匙
酒 1大匙
水 1/3杯

麵線(圖1) ....4兩(150公克)
九層塔 ....隨意

1 lb. (450g) live Manila
  clams or other shellfish

(1) 1 T. each, minced: ginger
  root, garlic cloves
1 minced chili pepper

(2) 1/4 t. each: salt, sugar
1 t. sesame oil
1 T. cooking wine
1/3 c. water

1/3 lb. (150g) noodle strings
  (Fig. 1)
fresh basil as desired

---

1 海瓜子刷洗乾淨，瀝乾備用。

2 油2大匙燒熱，炒香 **1** 料，隨入海瓜子及 **2** 料略炒(可蓋鍋)，將先開口的海瓜子逐一取出，全部開後，倒回炒拌均勻即可，九層塔可隨喜好加入。

3 多量水燒開，將麵線依包裝指示煮熟撈出置盤，再將煮好的海瓜子連汁倒入趁熱食用。

---

1 Scrub and wash clams; drain.

2 Heat 2 T. oil. Stir-fry **1** until fragrant; add clams and **2** ; stir briefly. Remove the opened clams during cooking. Return the removed clams when all shells in the wok are open; mix well. Sprinkle fresh basil if desired. Remove.

3 Bring a generous amount of water in a large pan to boil; cook noodle strings according to package directions. Remove and transfer to a plate. Pour juice with clam meat over the noodle strings. Serve hot.

---

*1 lb. (450g) almejas Manila
vivas u otro marisco*

(1) *1 C. c/u, finamente picado: raíz
de jengibre, diente de ajo
1 chile finamente picado*

(2) *1/4 c. c/u: sal, azúcar
1 c. aceite de sésamo
1 C. vino para cocinar
1/3 tz. agua*

*1/3 lb. (150g) fideos (Fig. 1)
albahaca fresca al gusto*

1 *Raspe y lave las almejas; escurra.*

2 *Caliente 2 C. de aceite. Fría-revolviendo* **1** *hasta que esté aromático; agregue las almejas y* **2** *; revuelva brevemente. Saque las almejas que se abrieron durante la cocción. Regrese estas almejas a la sartén wok cuando todas las conchas en la sartén se hayan abierto, mezcle bien. Si lo desea, cubra con albahaca fresca. Retire.*

3 *Haga hervir una gran cantidad de agua en una olla; cueza los fideos de acuerdo a las instrucciones del paquete. Retire y colóquelos en un plato. Vacíe el jugo con la carne de almeja sobre los fideos. Sirva caliente.*

1

海瓜子炒麵　　Fried Noodles & Clams
Tallarines Fritos y Almejas

海瓜子或其他貝類................
................12兩（450公克）
任何乾麵條(圖1) 4兩（150公克）
洋蔥(切絲)、番茄(切丁) ...共2杯

醬油 2大匙
糖 2/3大匙
鹽、麻油 各1/2小匙
高湯或水 1杯
太白粉 1大匙

蔥花 3大匙

🐚　🐚　🐚

1 lb. (450g) live Manila clams
　or other shellfish
1/3 lb. (150g) any dried
　noodles (Fig. 1)
2 c. total: shredded onion,
　chopped tomato

2 T. soy sauce
2/3 T. sugar
1/2 t. each: salt, sesame oil
1 c. stock or water
1 T. cornstarch

3 T. chopped green onions

🐚　🐚　🐚

*1 lb. (450g) almejas Manila
　vivas u otro marisco*
*1/3 lb. (150g) cualquier tallarín
　seco (Fig. 1)*
*2 tz. en total: cebolla rallada,
　tomate picado*

2 C. salsa de soya
2/3 C. azúcar
1/2 c. c/u: sal, aceite de sésamo
1 tz. caldo o agua
1 C. maicena

3 C. cebollín picado

1 海瓜子刷洗淨瀝乾，將麵條煮熟用冷水沖涼瀝乾重約12兩(450公克)。

2 油2大匙燒熱，先炒香洋蔥隨入番茄炒2分鐘，續入海瓜子及調勻的 ❶ 料燒開(可蓋鍋)，將先開口的海瓜子逐一取出，全部開後倒回再加麵條炒拌均勻，撒上蔥花即成。胡椒隨意。

🐚　🐚　🐚

1 Scrub and wash the clams; drain. Cook the noodles in boiling water; remove; rinse in cold water; drain. Noodles after cooked and drained weigh about 1 lb. (450g).

2 Heat 2 T. oil. Stir-fry onions until fragrant. Add tomatoes, stir 2 minutes. Stir in clams and mixture ❶; bring to a boil. Remove the opened clams during cooking; return the removed clams when all shells in the wok are open; mix well with noodles. Sprinkle with green onions or pepper as desired; serve.

🐚　🐚　🐚

1 *Raspe y lave las almejas; escurra. Cueza los tallarines en agua hirviendo; retire; enjuague en agua fría; escurra. Los tallarines después que se cuecen y se escurren pesan como 1 lb. (450g).*

2 *Caliente 2 C. de aceite. Fría las cebollas hasta que estén aromáticas. Agregue el tomate, revuelva por 2 minutos. Agregue revolviendo las almejas y la mezcla ❶; haga hervir. Saque las almejas que se abrieron durante la cocción; regrese estas almejas a la sartén wok cuando todas las conchas en la sartén se hayan abierto; mezcle bien con los tallarines. Espolvoree con cebollines o pimienta al gusto; sirva.*

1

鹹蜆

Almejas Marinadas

Marinated Clams

活蜆 ....半斤(300公克)
醬油 1/2杯
酒、冷開水 各1/4杯
醋、糖 各1/2杯
① 蒜(拍破) 5瓣
紅辣椒(切片) 1條
薑 4片

🐟 🐟 🐟

²/₃ lb. (300g) small live
   clams

¹/₂ c. soy sauce
① ¹/₄ c. each: cooking wine,
   cold water
¹/₂ c. each: vinegar, sugar
5 cloves of garlic, smashed
1 sliced red chili pepper
4 slices ginger root

🐟 🐟 🐟

²/₃ lb. (300g) almejas chicas
   vivas

¹/₂ tz. salsa de soya
① ¹/₄ tz. c/u: vino para cocinar,
   agua fría
¹/₂ tz. c/u: vinagre, azúcar
5 dientes de ajo, machacados
1 chile rojo rebanado
4 rebanadas raíz de jengibre

① 活蜆以清水泡數小時使其吐沙。

② 活蜆洗淨瀝乾，放入冰箱內冰凍，使用時取出使其自然解凍，等蜆開口時醃入 ① 料放入冰箱隔日即可食用，約可放置一星期。

☐ 鹹蜆已流行多年，其做法因時代不同有所改進，是很受歡迎的開胃菜。

🐟 🐟 🐟

1 Soak live clams in water several hours until the sand is released.

2 Wash, drain, and freeze the clams ahead of time. Thaw clams at room temperature before cooking. When clams are open, marinate in ①, and refrigerate overnight. Serve the next day. Marinated clams can be stored in refrigerator for up to one week.

☐ Marinated clams have been popular for many years. The marinating method has been improved over the years. They are a popular appetizer.

🐟 🐟 🐟

1 *Remoje las almejas vivas en agua por varias horas hasta que hayan soltado la arena.*

2 *Lave, escurra, y congele las almejas por adelantado. Descongele las almejas fuera del refrigerador antes de cocinar. Cuando se abran las almejas, marine en ①, y refrigere toda la noche. Sirva al día siguiente. Almejas marinadas se pueden mantener en el refrigerador por una semana.*

☐ *Almejas marinadas han sido populares por varios años. El método de marinar ha mejorado a través de los años. Es un aperitivo muy popular.*

檸汁生蠔　Oysters in Lemon Sauce
Ostiones en Salsa de Limón

活大生蠔(帶殼) 6個
酒 1大匙

檸檬汁 1大匙
薑汁 1小匙
鹽 ....¹⁄₆小匙或醬油 1大匙
蔥末 1大匙
辣椒粉 ....少許

🐌　🐌　🐌

**6 large oysters, live-in-shell
1 T. cooking wine**

**1 T. lemon juice
1 t. grated ginger root
¹/₆ t. salt, or 1 T. soy sauce
1 T. minced green onion
dash of paprika**

🐌　🐌　🐌

*6 ostiones grandes, vivos en su
　concha
1 C. vino para cocinar*

*1 C. jugo de limón
1 c. raíz de jengibre rallada
¹/₆ c. sal, ó 1 C. salsa de soya
1 C. cebollín finamente picado
pizca de paprika*

1 生蠔外殼刷洗乾淨，在殼連接處上方²/₃處用錐子鑽一個孔，再用起子伸入裡面將殼與生蠔密接的筋肉分離，即可將殼輕易打開(圖1,2)。

2 將生蠔肉取出沖洗，加酒1大匙醃5分鐘後瀝乾水份。

3 將生蠔肉放回殼內冰涼備用，食時淋上 ❶ 料；可當開胃菜。

☐ 沾料 ❶ 內，可隨意加番茄醬、芥末醬或白蘿蔔磨成泥。

🐌　🐌　🐌

1 Scrub and wash the shells of the oysters. Use an awl to make a hole at 2/3 of the joint end of the shell. Insert a screw driver into the hole until the adductor muscle is cut. Open the oyster shells (Figs. 1 & 2).

2 Take out the oyster meat and rinse. Marinate the meat in 1 T. cooking wine, 5 minutes; drain.

3 Return the meat to the shells and refrigerate. Just before serving, sprinkle with ❶. They can be served as an exotic appetizer.

☐ Ketchup, mustard, sauce, or turnip paste may be added into ❶ as a dip.

🐌　🐌　🐌

1 *Raspe y lave las conchas de los ostiones. Use un punzón para hacerle un hoyo a 2/3 de la conjuntura de la concha. Inserte un desarmador en el hoyo hasta que se corte el músculo aductor. Abra las conchas de los ostiones (Figs. 1 y 2).*

2 *Saque la carne de los ostiones y enjuague. Marínela en 1 C. de vino para cocinar, 5 minutos; escurra.*

3 *Regrese la carne a las conchas y refrigere. Poco antes de servir, espolvoree con ❶. Se pueden servir como un aperitivo exótico.*

☐ *Se puede agregar a ❶ catsup, mostaza, salsa, o nabo como dip.*

1

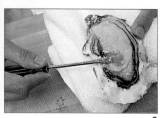

2

乾燒生蠔

Spicy Oysters

Ostiones Picantes

生蠔 ....半斤(300公克)

① 麵粉 3/4杯
發粉 1/2小匙

② 水 ....1/3杯，蛋 1個
鹽 1/4小匙

③ 蔥、薑、蒜末 各1/2大匙
辣豆瓣醬、酒釀(見20頁) ....
.............................各1大匙

④ 番茄醬 ....4大匙，鹽 ...1/4小匙
糖、太白粉 各1/2大匙
高湯或水 3/4杯

「炸油」 ....適量

2/3 lb. (300g) shucked
oysters

① 3/4 c. all-purpose flour
1/2 t. baking powder

② 1/3 c. water, 1 egg
1/4 t. salt

③ 1/2 T. each, minced: green
onion, ginger root, &
garlic cloves
1 T. each: chili bean paste,
sweet brewed rice (see
p. 20)

④ 4 T. ketchup, 1/4 t. salt
1/2 T. each: sugar, cornstarch
3/4 c. stock or water

oil for deep-frying

1️⃣ 生蠔洗淨，放入滾水內川燙1分鐘撈出瀝乾水份，輕拌麵粉1大匙。

2️⃣ 將 ① 料拌勻再拌入打勻的 ② 料成麵糊(太濃或太稀可酌加水或麵粉)。

3️⃣ 「炸油」燒熱，將生蠔拌麵糊逐一放入炸約2分鐘至金黃色撈出。

4️⃣ 油2大匙燒熱，炒香 ③ 料，隨入調勻的 ④ 料炒拌成濃汁倒入盤內，上置炸好的生蠔趁熱食用。

1️⃣ Wash raw oysters. Cook in boiling water for 1 minute; remove; drain; mix lightly with 1 T. flour.

2️⃣ Mix ① and ② separately and thoroughly. Combine mixtures ① and ②; stir to form a paste. (Add a little water if paste is too thick; add a little flour if paste is too thin.)

3️⃣ Heat oil for deep-frying. Coat the oysters with the paste. Drop them into oil, one by one; deep-fry 2 minutes until golden.

4️⃣ Heat the wok then add 2 T. oil. Stir-fry ③ until fragrant. Add mixture ④; cook until the liquid thickens. Pour into a plate. Top with the fried oysters. Serve hot.

2/3 lb. (300g) ostiones sin
concha

① 3/4 tz. harina
1/2 c. polvo de hornear

② 1/3 tz. agua, 1 huevo
1/4 c. sal

③ 1/2 C. c/u, finamente picado:
cebollín, raíz de jengibre, y
diente de ajo
1 C. c/u: pasta de frijol picante,
arroz fermentado dulce (vea
p. 20)

④ 4 C. catsup, 1/4 c. sal
1/2 C. c/u: azúcar, maicena
3/4 tz. caldo o agua

aceite para freír

1️⃣ *Lave los ostiones crudos. Cocine en agua hirviendo por 1 minuto; retire; escurra; mezcle ligeramente con 1 C. de harina.*

2️⃣ *Mezcle ① y ② por separado y completamente. Combine las mezclas ① y ②, bata formando una pasta. (Agregue un poco de agua si la pasta está muy espesa; agregue un poco de harina si la pasta está muy aguada.)*

3️⃣ *Caliente aceite para freír. Cubra los ostiones con la pasta. Suéltelos al aceite, uno por uno; fría por 2 minutos hasta que se doren.*

4️⃣ *Caliente la sartén wok luego agregue 2 C. de aceite. Fría-revolviendo ③ hasta que esté aromático. Agregue la mezcla ④, cocine hasta que el líquido se espese. Vacíe en un plato. Colóquele los ostiones fritos. Sirva caliente.*

豆豉生蠔　　Oysters & Bean Sauce

Ostiones en Salsa de Frijol

生蠔 ....12兩(450公克)

1
| 豆豉 2大匙
| 薑末 1/2大匙
| 蒜末 1大匙
| 辣椒(切片) 1條
| 蔥花 1/2杯

2
| 醬油 11/2大匙
| 蠔油、水 各1大匙
| 太白粉 1小匙

1 lb. (450g) shucked oysters

1
2 T. fermented black beans
1/2 T. minced ginger root
1 T. minced garlic
1 sliced red chili pepper

1/2 c. chopped green onions

2
11/2 T. soy sauce
1 T. each: oyster sauce,
　water
1 t. cornstarch

1 lb. (450g) ostiones sin concha

1
2 C. frijoles negros fermentados
1/2 C. raíz de jengibre finamente
　picada
1 C. ajo finamente picado
1 chile rojo rebanado

1/2 tz. cebollín picado

2
1 1/2 C. salsa de soya
1 C. c/u: salsa de ostión, agua
1 c. maicena

1 生蠔加少許鹽輕輕抓拌洗淨瀝乾。大的可略切，小的勿切，入滾水內燙20秒撈出瀝乾水份。

2 油2大匙燒熱，炒香 1 料，入生蠔略炒，再加蔥花及調勻的 2 料炒拌均勻即成。適合與飯配食。

1 Rub oysters with a pinch of salt; rinse; drain. Halve the oysters if they are too big. Blanch the oysters in boiling water for 20 seconds; remove and drain.

2 Heat 2 T. oil. Stir-fry 1 until fragrant. Stir in oysters briefly; add green onions and mixture 2; mix them well. Serve with rice.

1 *Frote los ostiones con una pizca de sal; enjuague; escurra. Corte los ostiones por la mitad, si son muy grandes. Sumerja los ostiones en agua hirviendo por 20 segundos; retire y escurra.*

2 *Caliente 2 C. de aceite. Fría-revolviendo 1 hasta que esté aromático. Agregue revolviendo los ostiones brevemente; agregue los cebollines y la mezcla 2; mezcle todo bien. Sirva con arroz.*

炒生蠔麵線　Noodle Strings & Oysters

Fideos y Ostiones

生蠔 ....6兩(225公克)
麵線 ....4兩(150公克)

①
蔥(6公分長) 10段
蒜、辣椒末 各1/2大匙
香菇(泡軟、切絲) 1/4杯

肉絲 ....1/2杯，醬油 1大匙

②
包心菜(切絲) 2杯
紅蘿蔔(切絲) 1/2杯

③
酒、醋 各1大匙
糖、鹽、麻油 各1/2小匙
高湯或水 ..1/2杯，胡椒 ....少許

🐌　🐌　🐌

1/2 lb. (225g) oysters
1/3 lb. (150g) thin noodles
(Somen)

①
10 green onion sections,
2 1/2" (6cm) long
1/2 T. each, minced: garlic
cloves, chili pepper
1/4 c. presoftened Chinese
black mushrooms,
shredded

1/2 c. meat shreds
1 T. soy sauce

②
2 c. shredded cabbage
1/2 c. shredded carrot

③
1 T. each: cooking wine,
vinegar
1/2 t. each: sugar, salt,
sesame oil
1/2 c. stock or water
pepper as desired

🐌　🐌　🐌

1/2 lb. (225g) ostiones
1/3 lb. (150g) fideo delgado
(Somen)

①
10 secciones de cebollines, 2 1/2''
(6cm) de largo
1/2 C. c/u, finamente picado:
dientes de ajo, chiles
1/4 tz. hongos negros chinos
ya ablandados, picados

1/2 tz. pedazos de carne
desmenuzada
1 C. salsa de soya

②
2 tz. repollo picado
1/2 tz. zanahoria rallada

③
1 C. c/u: vino para cocinar,
vinagre
1/2 c. c/u: azúcar, sal, aceite de
sésamo
1/2 tz. caldo o agua
pimienta al gusto

① 生蠔加少許鹽輕輕抓拌洗淨瀝乾。麵線依包裝指示煮熟後立即撈出用冷水沖涼瀝乾。

② 油3大匙燒熱，炒香 **①** 料，入肉絲及生蠔略炒，加醬油隨入 **②** 料及 **③** 料燒開，再加煮好的麵線炒拌均勻即成。

☐ 煮麵線時不可煮太爛，若麵線帶鹹，**③** 料內的鹽需酌量減少。

🐌　🐌　🐌

① Rub oysters gently with a pinch of salt; rinse and drain. Cook noodles according to package directions. Rinse noodles immediately under cold running water after being cooked; drain.

② Heat 3 T. oil. Stir-fry **①** until fragrant; add meat shreds and oysters; stir briefly; add soy sauce; stir in **②** and **③**; bring to a boil; mix well with cooked noodle strings. Serve.

☐ Don't overcook the noodle strings so they'll stay firm. Also, if noodle strings used contain salt, reduce salt in ingredient **③**.

🐌　🐌　🐌

① *Frote los ostiones ligeramente con una pizca de sal; enjuague y escurra. Cocine los fideos de acuerdo a las instrucciones del paquete. Enjuague los fideos en agua fría inmediatamente que se hayan cocido; escurra.*

② *Caliente 3 C. de aceite. Fría-revolviendo **①** hasta que esté aromático; agregue los pedazos de carne y los ostiones; revuelva brevemente; agregue la salsa de soya; agregue revolviendo **②** y **③** ; haga hervir; mezcle bien con los fideos cocidos. Sirva.*

☐ *No cocine de más los fideos para que se mantengan firmes. Además, si los fideos que usa ya llevan sal, reduzca la sal en los ingredientes de **③**.*

紙包海鮮   Seafood in Foil

Mariscos Envueltos en Aluminio 6人份・serves 6
6 porciones

中蝦 ....6兩(225公克)
生蠔 ....半斤(300公克)

酒 2大匙
鹽 1/4小匙
胡椒 ....少許

洋菇或草菇 12粒
筍、紅蘿蔔 各12片
菠菜 2棵

高湯或水 ..3大匙，鹽...1/3小匙
麻油 1/2大匙

鋁箔紙(30公分×30公分) ...6張

❧   ❧   ❧

¹/₂ lb. (225g) medium shrimp
²/₃ lb. (300g) oysters

2 T. cooking wine
¹/₄ t. salt
pepper as desired

12 mushrooms or straw
    mushrooms
12 slices each: bamboo
    shoots, carrot
2 bunches spinach

3 T. stock or water, ¹/₃ t. salt
¹/₂ T. sesame oil

6 sheets aluminum foil,
    12" x 12" (30cm x 30cm)

❧   ❧   ❧

¹/₂ lb. (225g) camarones
    medianos
²/₃ lb. (300g) ostiones

2 C. vino para cocinar
1/4 c. sal
pimienta al gusto

12 hongos u hongos con tallos
12 rebanadas c/u: brotes de
    bambú, zanahoria
2 racimos espinaca

3 C. caldo o agua, 1/3 c. sal
1/2 C. aceite de sésamo

6 hojas papel aluminio,
    12" x 12" (30cm x 30cm)

1

1 蝦去殼僅留尾，抽出腸泥。蝦及生蠔洗淨瀝乾後拌入 ❶ 料。

2 每張鋁箔紙放上1/6份的 ❷ 料、蝦、生蠔及調勻的 ❸ 料，包成鵝形或四方形 (圖1)的海鮮包備用。

3 烤箱燒至500°F(260°C)，將海鮮包放入烤18分鐘取出，連汁食用。

☐ 海鮮可用鮮魚肉、干貝，蔬菜可用蓮藕、芹菜、香菇等來取代。

❧   ❧   ❧

1 Shell the shrimp but leave tails intact. Devein the shrimp. Wash the shrimp and oysters; drain; mix in ❶ .

2 Divide ❷ into 6 portions. Put each portion, shrimp, oysters, and mixture ❸ on an aluminum foil. Wrap each foil into a swan or a square shape (Fig. 1); follow the same procedure to make 5 more; set aside.

3 Preheat oven to 500°F(260°C). Bake the wrapped seafood for 18 minutes. Serve liquid trapped inside the wrap with the seafood.

☐ Shrimp and oysters may be substituted by fresh fillet and scallops. Vegetables may be substituted with lotus roots, celery, and Chinese black mushrooms.

❧   ❧   ❧

1 *Pele los camarones pero deje la cola intacta. Desvene los camarones. Lave los camarones y ostiones; escurra; mezcle en ❶ .*

2 *Divida ❷ en 6 porciones. Coloque cada porción, camarones, ostiones, y la mezcla ❸ en un papel de aluminio. Envuelva cada aluminio en forma de cisne o cuadro (Fig. 1); siga el mismo procedimiento para hacer 5 más; deje aparte.*

3 *Precaliente el horno a 500°F (260°C). Hornee los mariscos envueltos por 18 minutos. Sirva el jugo que se formó en cada envoltura con los mariscos.*

☐ *Puede substituir los camarones y ostiones con filete fresco y escalopes. Los vegetales pueden ser substituidos por raíz de loto, apio, y hongos negros chinos.*

紅燒鮑魚　Abalone in Soy Sauce

Abulón en Salsa de Soya

宴客菜 · Serve at formal meal
Se sirve en una cena formal

鮑魚(切片) ....¹/₂罐
蔥(3公分長) 6段
薑 6片
① 香菇(泡軟)、筍 各8片

② 醬油 1¹/₂大匙
鮑魚罐汁 ....¹/₄杯
高湯或水 ....³/₄杯
麻油、糖 ....各¹/₂小匙
太白粉 1大匙

青花菜(燙熟) 8朵

ə̀ə ə̀ə ə̀ə

¹/₂ can abalone, sliced
6 green onion sections, 1¹/₄"
　(3cm) long
6 slices ginger root

① 8 slices each: pre-softened
　Chinese black mushrooms,
　bamboo shoots

② 1¹/₂ T. soy sauce
¹/₄ c. liquid from canned
　abalone
³/₄ c. stock or water
¹/₂ t. each: sesame oil, sugar
1 T. cornstarch

8 flowerets broccoli,
　blanched

ə̀ə ə̀ə ə̀ə

¹/₂ lata abulón, en rebanadas
6 secciones de cebollín, 1 ¹/₄"
　(3cm) de largo
6 rebanadas raíz de jengibre

① 8 rebanadas c/u: hongos negros
　chinos ablandados, brotes de
　bambú

② 1 ¹/₂ C. salsa de soya
¹/₄ tz. líquido de la lata de abulón
³/₄ tz. caldo o agua
¹/₂ c. aceite de sésamo, azúcar
1 C. maicena

8 florecillas de bróculi,
　sumergido en agua hirviendo

① 油2大匙燒熱，炒香蔥、薑，入 ① 料略炒，隨入調勻的 ② 料燒開成濃稠狀，再加鮑魚片拌勻置盤，以青花菜圍邊即成。

生菜鮑魚 ① 料可用草菇、毛菇來取代，青花菜亦可用青梗菜或生菜取代。

ə̀ə ə̀ə ə̀ə

① Heat 2 T. oil. Stir-fry green onions and ginger until fragrant. Add ①; stir briefly; add mixture ② ; bring to a boil; continue cooking until the juice thickens. Stir in sliced abalone; mix well; transfer to a plate. Arrange broccoli flowerets around the abalone on a plate. Serve.

Abalone & Lettuce Use straw mushrooms and mushrooms for ① , and bok choy or lettuce for broccoli. Other ingredients and procedures are the same as above.

ə̀ə ə̀ə ə̀ə

① Caliente 2 C. de aceite. Fría-revolviendo el cebollín y jengibre hasta que esté aromático. Agregue①; revuelva brevemente; agregue la mezcla ②; haga hervir; continúe cociendo hasta que el jugo espese. Agregue revolviendo las rebanadas de abulón; mezcle bien; vacíe en un plato. Acomode las florecillas de bróculi alrededor del abulón. Sirva.

Abulón y Lechuga Use hongos con tallos y hongos para ① , y bok choy o lechuga en lugar de bróculi. Los demás ingredientes y procedimientos son como los de esta receta.

生菜鮑魚 · Abalone & Lettuce
Abulón y Lechuga

奶汁鮑魚　　　Creamy Abalone

Abulón Cremoso

鮑魚(切片) ....¹/₂罐
洋蔥(切碎) ....¹/₂杯
紅蘿蔔、白花菜(均切塊)、洋菇
.........................各¹/₂杯
麵粉 1大匙
鮑魚罐汁 ....¹/₄杯
高湯 ......³/₄杯，胡椒 .....¹/₆小匙
鹽、糖 ....各¹/₂小匙
濃縮奶水或鮮奶 2大匙

¹/₂ can abalone, sliced
¹/₂ c. minced onion

¹/₂ c. each: carrot,
　cauliflower (both cut in
　pieces); mushrooms

1 T. all-purpose flour

¹/₄ c. liquid from canned
　abalone
³/₄ c. stock, ¹/₆ t. pepper
¹/₂ t. each: salt, sugar

2 T. evaporated milk or milk

¹/₂ *lata abulón, en rebanadas*
¹/₂ *tz. cebolla finamente picada*

¹/₂ *tz. c/u: zanahoria, coliflor
　(ambos cortados en pedazos);
　hongos*

1 *C. harina*

¹/₄ *tz. líquido de la lata de
　abulón*
³/₄ *tz. caldo, ¹/₆ c. pimienta*
¹/₂ *c. c/u: sal, azúcar*

2 *C. leche evaporada o leche*

1

2

1　油3大匙燒熱，炒香洋蔥，依序入 ❶ 料及麵粉略炒，續入 ❷ 料攪拌燒開，改小火蓋鍋煮5分鐘(中途須翻拌)，放入鮑魚片及奶水拌勻即成。

☐　如使用活鮑魚作菜時先取肉(圖1)去除內臟後洗淨切薄片(圖2)，加太白粉1大匙拌勻，將1/2杯油燒熱，入鮑魚片泡熟後使用。若是生吃，將鮑魚切片冰涼後沾沾料食用。

1　Heat 3 T. oil. Stir-fry the onions until fragrant; add ❶ in order listed then flour; stir briefly; pour in ❷; stir and cook until boiling. Reduce heat to low; continue cooking, covered, stirring halfway through 5 minute cooking. Pour in abalone and milk; mix well. Remove and serve.

☐　If using live abalone, take out meat (Fig. 1); remove internal organs; rinse; drain; slice into thin pieces (Fig. 2). Mix abalone slices well in 1 T. cornstarch. Heat 1/2 c. oil; cook abalone in hot oil until done. Serve. To eat raw abalone: slice raw abalone into thin pieces, refrigerate. Serve cold with the sauce as a dip.

1　*Caliente 3 C. de aceite. Fría-revolviendo la cebolla hasta que esté aromática; agregue ❶ en ese orden luego la harina; revuelva brevemente; vacíele ❷; revuelva y cocine hasta que hierva. Baje el fuego a bajo; continúe cocinando, tapado, mezclando cuando se haya cocido por la mitad de los 5 minutos requeridos. Vacíele el abulón y la leche; mezcle bien. Retire y sirva.*

☐　*Si se usa abulón vivo, sáquele la carne (Fig. 1); quítele los órganos internos; enjuague; escurra; rebane en rebanadas delgadas (Fig. 2). Mezcle las rebanadas de abulón bien en 1 C. de maicena. Caliente 1/2 tz. de aceite; cocine el abulón en el aceite caliente hasta que esté cocido. Sirva. Para comer abulón crudo: rebánelo en pedazos delgados, refrigere. Sirva frío con la salsa como dip.*

鮑魚冷盤

Abalone Cold Dish

Platillo Frío de Abulón

宴客菜・Serve at formal meal
Se sirve en una cena formal

鮑魚 1/2罐
芝麻醬或花生醬 1大匙
醬油 1大匙
沙拉醬(美乃滋) 4大匙
胡椒 1/8小匙

生菜 ....適量

❧ ❧ ❧

1/2 can abalone

**1 T. sesame paste or peanut
    butter   1 T.**
soy sauce
4 T. mayonnaise
1/8 t. pepper

lettuce as desired

❧ ❧ ❧

1/2 lata abulón

*1 C. pasta de sésamo o crema de
    cacahuate*
1 C. salsa de soya
4 C. mayonesa
1/8 c. pimienta

lechuga al gusto

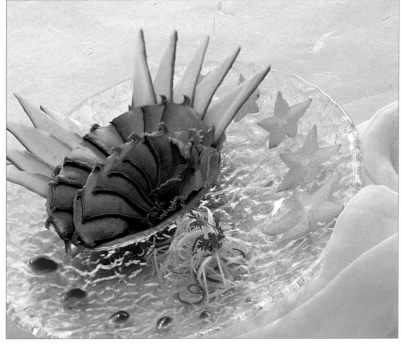

1 鮑魚切薄片。罐頭內的湯汁味鮮美可留做海鮮菜餚時使用。

2 將 ❶ 料攪拌成沾料。

3 生菜墊底,上置鮑魚片,沾沾料食用。此菜餚可用在宴客時當前菜。

❧ ❧ ❧

1 Cut abalone into thin slices. Reserve the delicious canned juice for other seafood recipes.

2 Stir and mix ❶; stir until blended into a dipping sauce.

3 Line the plate with lettuce then top with abalone slices. Serve with the dip. This may be served as an appetizer at a formal dinner.

❧ ❧ ❧

1 *Corte el abulón en rebanadas delgadas. Guarde el delicioso jugo de la lata para otras recetas de mariscos.*

2 *Revuelva y mezcle ❶; revuelva hasta que forme una salsa para dip.*

3 *Cubra el plato con lechuga y colóquele las rebanadas de abulón. Sirva con un dip. Se puede servir como aperitivo en una cena formal.*

五味九孔 / Flavored Abalone

Abulón Preparado

宴客菜 · Serve at formal meal
Se sirve en una cena formal

九孔 ....12兩(450公克)

番茄醬 2大匙
醬油、黑醋 各1大匙
糖 ....¹/₂ 大匙

蔥、薑、蒜、辣椒末 ...各1小匙

水 ....1杯，糖 1¹/₃大匙
醬油、酒 各2大匙

檸檬汁或醋 ....¹/₂ 大匙
麻油 ....¹/₂ 大匙

🦐　🦐　🦐

1 lb. (450g) abalone (chiu kung)

2 T. ketchup
1 T. each: soy sauce; black vinegar
¹/₂ T: sugar

1 t. each (minced): green onions, ginger root, garlic cloves, and chili pepper

1 c. water, 1¹/₃ T. sugar
2 T. each: soy sauce, cooking wine

¹/₂ T. lemon juice or vinegar
¹/₂ T. sesame oil

🦐　🦐　🦐

1 lb. (450g) abulón (chiu kung)

2 C. catsup
1 C. c/u: salsa de soya, vinagre negro
¹/₂ C. azúcar

1 c. c/u: (finamente picado): cebollín, raíz de jengibre, diente de ajo, y chiles

1 tz. agua, 1¹/₃ C. azúcar
2 C. c/u: salsa de soya, vino para cocinar

¹/₂ C. jugo de limón o vinagre
¹/₂ C. aceite de sésamo

1 刷子沾少許鹽，刷洗九孔肉部黏液及外殼，並沖洗乾淨。

2 大量水燒開，將九孔放入燙2分鐘至熟，待冷。為求美觀可將九孔肉翻面再置回殼內，食時淋入 **1** 料即成。

紅燒九孔 油燒熱，炒香 **2** 料，九孔肉朝下煎成金黃色，隨入 **3** 料燒開煮至汁收乾約8分鐘，再加 **4** 料拌勻。也可用鳳螺，其燒煮方法同。

🦐　🦐　🦐

1 Scrub sticky debris off abalone meat and shells with a brush dipped with some salt. Rinse and drain.

2 Bring a pot of water to boil; add in the abalone and cook for 2 minutes until done. Let cool. For better presentation, turn the meat over and put on the shell. Serve with **1** .

Chiu Kung in Soy Sauce Heat oil; stir-fry **2** until fragrant. Fry abalone, meat side down, until golden. Add **3** and bring to a boil; continue to cook 8 minutes until liquid is almost evaporated. Add **4** ; stir to mix well. Periwinkle may be cooked in the same way.

🦐　🦐　🦐

1 *Raspando con una brocha sumergida en sal, quite el escombro pegajoso de la carne de abulón y las conchas. Enjuague y escurra.*

2 *Haga hervir una olla de agua; agréguele el abulón y cocine por 2 minutos hasta que esté cocido. Deje enfriar. Para una mejor presentación, voltee la carne y colóquela en la concha. Sirva con* **1** *.*

Chiu Kung en Salsa de Soya *Caliente aceite; fría-revolviendo* **2** *hasta que esté aromático. Fría el abulón, lado de la carne hacía abajo, hasta que esté dorado. Agregue* **3** *y haga hervir; continúe cocinando por 8 minutos hasta que el líquido casi se haya evaporado. Agregue* **4** *; revuelva mezclando bien. Vincapervinca se puede preparar de la misma forma.*

紅燒九孔 · Chiu Kung in Soy Sauce
Chiu Kung en Salsa de Soya

上湯九孔　Abalone in Stock

Abulón en Caldo

宴客菜・Serve at formal meal
Se sirve en una cena formal

九孔 ....12兩(450公克)

① 蔥末 2大匙
　 薑末 1大匙

② 高湯 1杯
　 酒 3大匙
　 鹽、糖 各1/2小匙
　 胡椒 1/8小匙
　 太白粉 1大匙

麻油 1小匙

🦐　🦐　🦐

1 lb. (450g) abalone (chiu kung)

① 2 T. minced green onion
　 1 T. minced ginger root

② 1 c. stock
　 3 T. cooking wine
　 1/2 t. each: salt, sugar
　 1/8 t. pepper
　 1 T. cornstarch

1 t. sesame oil

🦐　🦐　🦐

1 lb. (450g) abulón (chiu kung)

① *2 C. cebollín finamente picado*
　 1 C. raíz de jengibre finamente picada

② *1 tz. caldo*
　 3 C. vino para cocinar
　 1/2 c. c/u: sal, azúcar
　 1/8 c. pimienta
　 1 C. maicena

1 c. aceite de sésamo

1. 刷子沾少許鹽，刷洗九孔肉部黏液及外殼，並沖洗乾淨。

2. 油2大匙燒熱，九孔肉朝下煎成金黃色鏟於鍋邊，隨入 ① 料炒香，再加 ② 料並將九孔鏟回鍋中蓋鍋燜煮4分鐘，灑上麻油即成。

上湯龍蝦　將龍蝦頭與身相連接之薄膜劃開後扭轉拉開，抽出腸泥洗淨，由分節處切塊，每塊再切半。其做法參考上面 2。

🦐　🦐　🦐

1. Scrub sticky debris off abalone meat and shells with a brush dipped with some salt. Rinse and drain.

2. Heat 2 T. oil. Pan-fry abalone, meat side down, until golden; move to the side of the wok. Add ①, stir-fry until fragrant. Add ②; spatula abalone to the center of the wok; cook, covered, 4 minutes. Sprinkle with sesame oil.

Lobster in Stock　Cut at the joint of the head and body; twist off the head and pull the head and body apart. Devein. Wash then drain. Cut lobster at the joints. Then cut each piece in half. Cook as directed in Step 2, above.

🦐　🦐　🦐

1. *Raspando con una brocha sumergida en sal, quite el escombro pegajoso de la carne de abulón y las conchas. Enjuague y escurra.*

2. *Caliente 2 C. de aceite. Sofría el abulón, lado de la carne hacia abajo, hasta que esté dorado; haga a un lado de la sartén wok. Agregue ①, fría revolviendo hasta que esté aromático. Agregue ②; con una espátula mueva el abulón al centro de la sartén; cocine, tapado, por 4 minutos. Rocíe con aceite de sésamo.*

Langosta en Caldo　*Corte en la coyuntura de la cabeza y el cuerpo; retuerza la cabeza y sepárela del cuerpo. Desvene. Lave y escurra. Corte la langosta en las coyunturas. Luego corte cada pedazo por la mitad. Cocine siguiendo las instrucciones del paso 2 de arriba.*

上湯龍蝦・Lobster in Stock
Langosta en Caldo

生吃九孔　　Abalone & Mustard Sauce

Abulón en Salsa de Mostaza

宴客菜 · Serve at formal meal
Se sirve en una cena formal

九孔 ....12兩(450公克)
白蘿蔔絲 1杯

山葵醬 ....適量
醬油 2大匙

⁂　⁂　⁂

1 lb. (450g) abalone (chiu
　kung)
1 c. shredded white radish

Japanese horse radish
　paste (wasabi) as desired
2 T. soy sauce

⁂　⁂　⁂

*1 lb. (450g) abulón (chiu kung)
1 tz. rábano blanco rallado*

*pasta de rábano picante japonés
　(wasabi) al gusto
2 C. salsa de soya*

1 將九孔肉取出洗淨，切薄片，內臟燙熟。白蘿蔔絲泡冰水10分鐘備用。

2 將九孔肉及白蘿蔔絲裝盤，沾調勻的 **1** 料食用。

⁂　⁂　⁂

1 Remove the abalone meat; wash and drain. Slice the meat into thin pieces. Cook the internal organs in boiling water until done. Soak shredded white radish in ice water for 10 minutes; remove and drain.

2 Place the abalone on a bed of shredded white radish. Serve with mixture **1** as a dip.

⁂　⁂　⁂

1 *Saque la carne de abulón; lave y escurra. Rebane la carne en rebanadas delgadas. Cocine los órganos interiores en agua hirviendo. Remoje el rábano rallado en agua helada por 10 minutos; retire y escurra.*

2 *Coloque el abulón sobre una capa de rábano rallado. Sirva con la mezcla **1** como dip.*

蠔油鮮貝　Scallops in Oyster Sauce
Escalopes en Salsa de Ostiones

大鮮貝* ....半斤(300公克)
1. 酒、太白粉 各1大匙
   鹽 1/4小匙
2. 蠔油 1大匙
   高湯或水 1/4杯
   太白粉 1/2小匙
   麻油 1/4小匙
   蔥末(無亦可) 1大匙

ɞ   ɞ   ɞ

2/3 lb. (300g) fresh large
scallops*

1. 1 T. each: cooking wine,
   cornstarch
   1/4 t. salt

2. 1 T. oyster sauce
   1/4 c. stock or water
   1/2 t. cornstarch
   1/4 t. sesame oil

   1 T. minced green onion
   (optional)

ɞ   ɞ   ɞ

2/3 lb. (300g) escalopes grandes
frescos*

1. 1 C. c/u: vino para cocinar,
   maicena
   1/4 c. sal

2. 1 C. salsa de ostiones
   1/4 tz. caldo o agua
   1/2 c. maicena
   1/4 c. aceite de sésamo

   1 C. cebollín finamente picado
   (opcional)

---

1 鮮貝洗淨拭乾，在兩面切網狀，深至1/4處(圖1)加 ❶ 料拌勻備用。

2 油1大匙燒熱，大火將鮮貝兩面煎黃約2分鐘，再加調勻的 ❷ 料及蔥末炒拌均勻即成。

★ 若使用冷凍鮮貝，需在 ❶ 料內多加小蘇打1/4小匙，防止煎時縮小。

ɞ   ɞ   ɞ

1 Wash scallops, drain, and pat dry. Cut 1/4 of the depth on both sides to form crisscross cuts (Fig. 1); mix well in ❶; set aside.

2 Heat 1 T. oil. Pan-fry scallops until golden on both sides, 2 minutes. Add mixture ❷ and green onions; mix well. Serve.

★ If frozen scallops are used, add 1/4 t. baking soda in ❶ to prevent shrinking during cooking.

ɞ   ɞ   ɞ

1 *Lave los escalopes, escurra, y seque ligeramente. Corte 1/4 parte de la profundidad de ambos lados para formar cortadas en forma de equis (Fig. 1); mezcle bien en ❶ ; deje aparte.*

2 *Caliente 1 C. de aceite. Sofría los escalopes hasta que se doren por ambos lados, 2 minutos. Agregue la mezcla ❷ y el cebollín; mezcle bien. Sirva.*

★ *Si usa escalopes congelados, agregue 1/4 c. de bicarbonato en ❶ para que no se encojan al cocinar.*

1

魚香鮮貝　Spicy Scallops

Escalopes Picantes

2人份・Serves 2
2 porciones

大鮮貝* ....6兩(225公克)

酒、太白粉 各1大匙
鹽 1/6小匙

辣豆瓣醬 1小匙
蔥、薑、蒜末 各1大匙

洋菇(切半)、小黃瓜(切片)共2杯

水 ....3大匙，醋 1/2大匙
醬油 11/2大匙
糖、麻油、太白粉 各1小匙

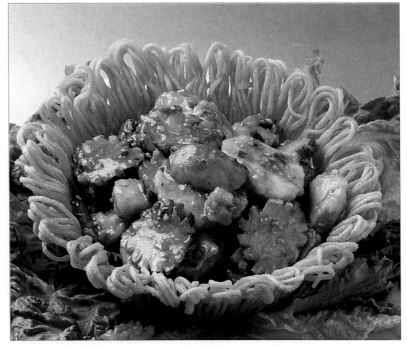

1 鮮貝洗淨拭乾，橫切2片，調入 **1** 料再拌油1大匙較容易炒開。

2 油2大匙燒熱，入鮮貝煎炒至金黃色(圖1)撈出，擦乾鍋面。

3 油2大匙燒熱，炒香 **2** 料，隨入 **3** 料略炒再加調勻的 **4** 料及鮮貝炒勻即可。

★ 若使用冷凍鮮貝，需在 **1** 料內多加小蘇打1/4小匙，防止煎時縮小。

1/2 lb. (225g) fresh large scallops*

1 1 T. each: cooking wine, cornstarch
1/6 t. salt

2 1 t. chili bean paste
1 T. each (minced): green onion, ginger root, garlic cloves

3 2 c. total: halved mushrooms, sliced cucumber

4 3 T. water, 1/2 T. vinegar
11/2 T. soy sauce
1 t. each: sugar, sesame oil, cornstarch

---

1 Wash scallops, drain, and pat dry. Cut scallops widthwise into 2 pieces. Add **1** then 1 T. oil to separate scallops easily during stir-frying.

2 Heat 2 T. oil. Pan-fry scallops until golden (Fig. 1); remove; Wipe wok dry.

3 Heat 2 T. oil; stir-fry **2** until fragrant. Add **3**; stir briefly; stir in mixture **4** and scallops until well mixed. Serve.

★ If scallops are frozen, add 1/4 t. baking soda in **1** to prevent shrinking during cooking.

---

*1/2 lb. (225g) escalopes grandes frescos***

1 1 C. c/u: vino para cocinar, maicena
1/6 c. sal

2 1 c. pasta de frijol picante
1 C. c/u, finamente picado: cebollín, raíz de jengibre, diente de ajo

3 2 tz. en total: hongos cortados a la mitad, pepino rebanado

4 3 C. agua, 1/2 C. vinagre
11/2 C. salsa de soya
1 c. c/u: azúcar, aceite de sésamo, maicena

---

1 *Lave los escalopes, escurra, y seque ligeramente. Corte los escalopes a lo ancho en 2 pedazos. Agregue* **1** *luego 1 C. de aceite para que los escalopes se separen fácilmente cuando se fríen-revolviendo.*

2 *Caliente 2 C. de aceite. Sofría los escalopes hasta que se doren (Fig. 1); retire; seque y limpie la sartén wok.*

3 *Caliente 2 C. de aceite; fría-revolviendo* **2** *hasta que esté aromático. Agregue* **3**; *revuelva brevemente; agregue revolviendo la mezcla* **4** *y los escalopes hasta que estén bien mezclados. Sirva.*

★ *Si usa escalopes congelados, agregue 1/4 c. de bicarbonato en* **1** *para que no se encojan al cocinar.*

1

白灼象拔蚌　　**Boiled Geoduck Clam**

Almeja Geoduck Hervida

活象拔蚌1個 ...1斤半(900公克)
醬油 1/3杯

① 蔥、薑(切絲) 各2大匙
乾辣椒(切段) 1條
香菜(無亦可) 1大匙

🐌　🐌　🐌

1 live geoduck clam, about
2 lbs. (900g)
1/3 c. soy sauce

① 2 T. each: shredded green
　onion, ginger root
1 dried chili pepper, cut
　into sections
1 T. coriander (optional)

🐌　🐌　🐌

1 almeja geoduck viva, como
　2 lbs. (900g)
1/3 tz. salsa de soya

2 C. c/u: cebollín y raíz de
　jengibre ralladas
1 chile seco cortado en
　secciones
1 C. cilantro (opcional)

1 象拔蚌除去外殼及內臟(圖1)，再將象鼻部份用滾水略燙，去除外面的硬薄皮，再切大薄片(使用的部份僅為全重的1/3)。

2 將醬油放入碗內，上擺 ① 料，淋上燒滾的沙拉油3大匙即成沾料。

3 水燒開，入象拔蚌燙熟約20秒撈出置盤，趁熱沾沾料食用。湯汁可留做他用。如用魷魚即為白灼魷片。

🐌　🐌　🐌

1 Remove and discard the shell and the internal organs of the clam (Fig. 1). Blanch the clam in boiling water then remove the skin; cut into large thin slices. (The clam used is about 1/3 of the entire weight.)

2 To make the dip, pour soy sauce into a bowl; put ① on top; pour on 3 T. hot boiling oil.

3 Bring water to boil; cook clam 20 seconds until done. Transfer it to a plate. Serve hot with dip. Reserve the stock for other uses. To make "Boiled Squid", use squid in place of clam.

🐌　🐌　🐌

1 *Quite y tire a la basura la concha y los órganos internos de la almeja (Fig. 1). Sumerja la almeja en agua hirviendo luego quítele la piel; corte en rebanadas delgadas. (La almeja que se usa es como 1/3 de todo su peso.)*

2 *Para preparar el dip, vacíe la salsa de soya en un tazón; coloque ① encima; vacíele 3 C. de aceite caliente.*

3 *Haga hervir el agua; cocine la almeja por 20 segundos hasta que este cocida. Coloque en un plato. Sirva caliente con el dip. Guarde el caldo para otro uso. Para preparar "Calamar Hervido," use calamar en lugar de almeja.*

1

生炒象拔蚌　　Fried Geoduck Clam

Almeja Geoduck Frita

宴客菜 · Serve at formal meal
Se sirve en una cena formal

象拔蚌(淨肉) ......6兩(225公克)
蔥(3公分長) 6段
薑 6片
紅蘿蔔、草菇或洋菇...............
...................................切片共2杯
水 3大匙
酒 1/2大匙
鹽、糖 各1/3小匙
麻油、太白粉 各1小匙
胡椒 ....少許

🦐　🦐　🦐

**1/2 lb. (225g) shelled
geoduck clam**

**6 green onion sections,
1 1/4" (3cm) long
6 ginger slices**

**2 c. total: carrots, straw
mushrooms or
mushrooms**

**3 T. water
1/2 T. cooking wine
1/3 t. each: salt, sugar
1 t. each: sesame oil,
cornstarch
pepper as desired**

🦐　🦐　🦐

*1/2 lb. (225g) almeja geoduck
sin concha*

*6 secciones de cebollín, 1 1/4"
(3cm) de largo
6 rebanadas de jengibre*

*2 tz. en total: zanahorias,
hongos con tallo u hongos*

*3 C. agua
1/2 C. vino para cocinar
1/3 c. c/u: sal, azúcar
1 c. c/u: aceite de sésamo,
maicena
pimienta al gusto*

1 將象拔蚌切大薄片，入滾水內燙熟約20秒撈出。

2 油2大匙燒熱，炒香 **1** 料，入 **2** 料略炒，隨入象拔蚌翻炒，再加調勻的 **3** 料炒拌均勻即成。

☐ 若無象拔蚌可用其他鮮貝肉取代。

🦐　🦐　🦐

1 Slice the clam meat into large thin pieces; blanch in boiling water 20 seconds until done; remove.

2 Heat 2 T. oil. Stir-fry **1** until fragrant. Add **2**; stir-fry briefly. Stir in the clam then mixture **3** quickly until combined. Serve.

☐ Geoduck clam may be substituted with fresh scallops.

🦐　🦐　🦐

1 *Rebane la carne de almeja en pedazos delgados; sumerja en agua hirviendo por 20 segundos hasta que esté cocida; retire.*

2 *Caliente 2 C. de aceite. Fría-revolviendo **1** hasta que esté aromático. Agregue **2** ; fría-revolviendo brevemente. Agregue mezclando la almeja luego la mezcla **3** rápidamente hasta que se combine. Sirva.*

☐ *Almeja geoduck puede substituirse por escalopes frescos.*

生炒牛角蚌
Escalopes Sofritos

Fried Scallops

活牛角蚌 12個

① 酒、太白粉 各1大匙
   鹽 ....¹/₆小匙

② 紅辣椒(切片) 1條
   蔥 6段
   薑 6片
   蒜末 1小匙

③ 紅蘿蔔、碗豆莢 各12片
   草菇 12個

④ 水..........3大匙，鹽 ....¹/₃小匙
   麻油、太白粉 各1小匙

🐚 🐚 🐚

12 scallops, live-in-shell

① **1 T. each: cooking wine,**
   cornstarch
   ¹/₆ t. salt

② **1 sliced red chili pepper**
   6 each: green onion
   sections, ginger slices
   1 t. minced garlic cloves

③ **12 each: carrot slices,**
   Chinese snow peas
   12 straw mushrooms

④ **3 T. water, ¹/₃ t. salt**
   1 t. each: sesame oil,
   cornstarch

🐚 🐚 🐚

12 escalopes, vivos en su
concha

① *1 C. c/u: vino para*
   cocinar, maicena
   ¹/₆ c. sal

② *1 chile rojo rebanado*
   6 c/u: secciones de
   cebollín, rebanadas de
   jengibre
   1 c. diente de ajo finamente
   picado

③ *12 c/u: rebanadas de*
   zanahoria, chícharos chinos
   12 hongos con tallo

④ *3 C. agua, ¹/₃ c. sal*
   1 c. c/u: aceite de
   sésamo, maicena

1️⃣ 牛角蚌（見右頁，✳）；取肉去內臟，洗淨，切成兩片調入 ① 料。

2️⃣ 油2大匙燒熱，入牛角蚌煎炒至變白撈出，擦乾鍋面。

3️⃣ 油2大匙燒熱，炒香 ② 料，隨入 ③ 料略炒，再加調勻的 ④ 料及牛角蚌炒拌均勻即成。

🐚 🐚 🐚

1️⃣ Shuck scallops (see p. 61, ✳) ; remove their insides then wash and drain. Cut the scallops in half; marinate in ① .

2️⃣ Heat 2 T. oil. Fry scallops until they turn white; remove. Wipe wok dry.

3️⃣ Heat the wok then add 2 T. oil. Stir-fry ② until fragrant; add ③ ; stir briefly. Stir in mixture ④ and scallops until well mixed. Serve.

🐚 🐚 🐚

1️⃣ *Desconche los escalopes (vea p. 61, ✳);quíteles las entrañas luego lave y escurra.Corte los escalopes por la mitad;marine en ① .*

2️⃣ *Caliente 2C.de aceite.Fría los escalopes hasta que se pongan blancos;retire. Limpie y seque la sartén wok.*

3️⃣ *Caliente la sartén wok luego agregue 2C.de aceite. Fría-revolviendo ② hasta que esté aromático; agregue③ ; revuelva brevemente.Agregue revolviendo la mezcla ④ y los escalopes hasta que esté bien mezclado. Sirva.*

清蒸牛角蚌

Steamed Scallops
Escalopes al Vapor

宴客菜・Serve at formal meal
Se sirve en una cena formal

活牛角蚌 12個
酒、醬油 各1/2大匙
麻油 1小匙
鹽 1/6小匙
胡椒 ....少許

嫩薑絲 1大匙
紅辣椒(切絲) 1條
蒜末 1/2大匙

🐟 　🐟 　🐟

12 scallops, live-in-shell

**¹/₂ T. each: cooking wine,
　soy sauce
1 t. sesame oil
¹/₆ t. salt
pepper as desired**

**1 T. shredded baby ginger
　root
1 shredded chili pepper
¹/₂ T. minced garlic cloves**

🐟 　🐟 　🐟

*12 escalopes vivos en su
　concha*

*¹/₂ C. c/u: vino para cocinar,
　salsa de soya
1 c. aceite de sésamo
¹/₆ c. sal
pimienta al gusto*

*1 C. raíz de jengibre tierna
　rallada
1 chile picado
¹/₂ C. diente de ajo finamente
　picado*

1 牛角蚌取肉去內臟洗淨拭乾，調入 **1** 料，放回殼內再撒上 **2** 料。

2 水燒開，大火蒸5分鐘至剛熟，趁熱食用。

★ 牛角蚌(圖1)為一種極美味之鮮貝，此道菜適於宴客用，如無牛角蚌可用其他鮮貝取代。

🐟 　🐟 　🐟

1 Shuck scallops; wash and pat dry; mix in **1**. Return each scallop to its shell; sprinkle with **2**.

2 Steam the scallops over boiling water for 5 minutes or until just done. Serve hot.

★ The scallops in Fig. 1 are very delicious. This dish is suitable for a formal dinner. If the scallops in Fig. 1 are not available, use other fresh scallops for the recipe.

🐟 　🐟 　🐟

1 *Desconche los escalopes; lave y seque ligeramente; mezcle en **1**. Regrese cada escalope a su concha; espolvoree con **2**.*

2 *Cocine los escalopes al vapor sobre agua hirviendo por 5 minutos o hasta que estén cocidos. Sirva caliente.*

★ *Los escalopes en Fig. 1 son muy deliciosos. Este platillo es apropiado para una cena formal. Si no encuentra los escalopes de Fig. 1, use otros escalopes frescos para esta receta.*

1

清蒸蟹
Steamed Crab

Cangrejo al Vapor

活蟹 ....1斤半(900公克)

①
蔥 2支
薑 2片
酒 1大匙
鹽 1/8小匙

②
醋 3大匙
鹽 1/8小匙
薑(切碎) 1大匙

⅔   ⅔   ⅔

2 lbs. (900g) crab, live-in-
shell

①
2 green onions
2 slices ginger root
1 T. cooking wine
1/8 t. salt

②
3 T. vinegar
1/8 t. salt
1 T. minced ginger root

⅔   ⅔   ⅔

*2 lbs. (900g) cangrejo, vivo en
su carapacho*

①
*2 cebollines
2 rebanadas raíz de jengibre
1 C. vino para cocinar
1/8 c. sal*

②
*3 C. vinagre
1/8 c. sal
1 C. raíz de jengibre finamente
picada*

1 蟹處理乾淨，瀝乾後淨重約1斤(600公克)，蟹處理法見9頁；拌入 **①** 料備用。

2 水燒開，將處理好的蟹放入蒸鍋大火蒸10分鐘至熟，切塊置盤，沾 **②** 料食用。

⅔   ⅔   ⅔

1 Prepare the crab (see p. 9); wash and drain. The crab after preparation should weigh 1 1/3 lbs. (600g). Mix well in **①**.

2 Bring water to boil; steam crab over high heat until done, 10 minutes. Cut crab in pieces and place on a plate. Serve **②** as a dip.

⅔   ⅔   ⅔

1 *Prepare el cangrejo (vea p. 9); lave y escurra. Después de prepararse el cangrejo debe pesar 1 1/3 lb. (600g). Mezcle bien en **①**.*

2 *Haga hervir el agua; cocine el cangrejo al vapor sobre fuego alto hasta que esté cocido, 10 minutos. Corte el cangrejo en pedazos y coloque en un plato. Sirva **②** como dip.*

蔥油蟹

Crab & Green Onions

Cangrejo y Cebollines

2人份 · serves 2
2 porciones

活蟹 …………1斤半(900公克)	
辣椒(切絲) ………………1支	
蔥絲 …………………4大匙	
薑絲 …………………2大匙	
胡椒 …………………1/8小匙	
醬油 …………………1小匙	
高湯或水 …………………1/2杯	
麻油 …………………1小匙	
鹽 …………………1/2小匙	

🦐   🦐   🦐

2 lbs. (900g) crab, live-in-shell

1 shredded chili pepper
4 T. shredded green onions
2 T. shredded ginger root
1/8 t. pepper

1 t. soy sauce

1/2 c. stock or water
1 t. sesame oil
1/2 t. salt

🦐   🦐   🦐

2 lbs. (900g) cangrejo, vivo en su carapacho

1 chile picado
4 C. cebollín picado
2 C. raíz de jengibre rallada
1/8 c. pimienta

1 c. salsa de soya

1/2 tz. caldo o agua
1 c. aceite de sésamo
1/2 c. sal

1 蟹處理乾淨，瀝乾後淨重約1斤(600公克)，蟹處理法見9頁。

2 水燒開，將處理好的蟹放入蒸鍋大火蒸10分鐘至熟，切塊置盤，上擺 **1** 料及醬油，淋入燒開的 **2** 料即成。

🦐   🦐   🦐

1 Prepare the crab (see p. 9); wash and drain. The crab after preparation should weigh 1 1/3 lbs. (600g).

2 Bring water to boil; steam the crab over high heat until done, about 10 minutes. Remove; cut into pieces and arrange on a plate; pour **1** and soy sauce on top. Bring **2** to a boil then pour over the crab; serve.

🦐   🦐   🦐

1 *Prepare el cangrejo (vea p. 9); después de prepararse el cangrejo debe pesar 1 1/3 lbs. (600g).*

2 *Haga hervir el agua; cocine el cangrejo al vapor sobre fuego alto hasta que esté cocido, por 10 minutos. Retire; corte en pedazos y acomode en un plato; vacíe **1** y la salsa de soya encima. Haga hervir **2** luego vacíe sobre el cangrejo; sirva.*

活蟹 ....1斤半(900公克)
太白粉 3大匙

① 蔥(3公分長) 12段
薑 12片

② 酒 2大匙
高湯或水 1杯
鹽、糖 ....各¹/₂小匙
胡椒 ....¹/₈小匙
麻油 1小匙
太白粉 1大匙

☙ ☙ ☙

2 lbs. (900g) crab, live-in-shell
3 T. cornstarch

① 12 sections green onion,
1 ¹/₄" (3cm) long
12 slices ginger root

② 2 T. cooking wine
1 c. stock or water
¹/₂ t. each: salt, sugar
¹/₈ t. pepper
1 t. sesame oil
1 T. cornstarch

☙ ☙ ☙

2 lbs.(900g)cangrejo, vivo en
su carapacho
3 C. maicena

① 12 secciones de cebollín,
1¹/₄"(3cm) de largo
12 rebanadas raíz de jengibre

② 2 C. vino para cocinar
1 tz. caldo agua
¹/₂ c. c/u: sal, azucar
¹/₈ c. pimieta
1 c. aceite de sésamo
1 C. maicena

芙蓉炒蟹 · Crab & Egg White
Cangrejo y Clara de Huevo

① 蟹處理乾淨，瀝乾切塊後淨重約1斤(600公克)，蟹處理法見9頁，拌入太白粉備用。

② 油3大匙燒熱，將蟹兩面煎呈金黃色，略加油炒香 **①** 料，再入調勻的 **②** 料燒開後，蓋鍋續煮2分鐘(中途略炒拌)至蟹肉熟且汁呈濃狀即成。

芙蓉炒蟹 將煮好的蔥薑炒蟹加入2個打散的蛋白，炒至蛋剛凝固即成。

☙ ☙ ☙

① Prepare the crab (see p. 9); wash and drain; cut in pieces. The crab after preparation should weigh 1 1/3 lbs. (600g). Coat crab with cornstarch.

② Heat 3 T. oil. Pan-fry crab until golden on both sides. Add a little more oil and stir-fry **①** until fragrant. Stir in mixture **②** ; bring to a boil. Continue cooking, covered; stir lightly during cooking, until done or until juice thickens, about 2 minutes.

Crab & Egg White Add 2 beaten egg whites to the above cooked dish in the wok. Stir-fry until the egg whites are just set. Serve.

☙ ☙ ☙

① *Prepare el cangrejo (vea p. 9); lave y escurra; corte en pedazos. Después de prepararse el cangrejo debe pesar 1 1/3 lbs. (600g). Reboce el cangrejo con maicena.*

② *Caliente 3 C. de aceite. Sofría el cangrejo hasta que esté dorado por ambos lados. Agregue un poco más de aceite y fría-revolviendo **①** hasta que esté aromático. Agregue revolviendo la mezcla **②** ; haga hervir. Continúe cocinando, tapado; revuelva ligeramente durante la cocción, hasta que esté cocido o hasta que el líquido espese, como 2 minutos.*

Cangrejo y Clara de Huevo *Agregue 2 claras de huevos batidas al platillo de arriba , cocido en la sartén wok. Fría-revolviendo hasta que las claras de huevos se cuajen. Sirva.*

豉汁炒蟹　Crab & Bean Sauce

Cangrejo y Salsa de Frijol

活蟹 ....1斤半(900公克)
太白粉 3大匙

蔥、薑、蒜末 各1/2大匙
豆豉(切碎) 1 1/2大匙

酒 2大匙
高湯或水 1杯
醬油或蠔油 1大匙
鹽 .....1/4小匙，糖 1/2小匙
胡椒 ....1/8小匙，麻油 1小匙
太白粉 1大匙

🦐　　🦐　　🦐

2 lbs. (900g) crab, live-in-shell
3 T. cornstarch

1/2 T. each, minced: green onion, ginger root, garlic cloves
1 1/2 T. fermented black beans, minced

2 T. cooking wine
1 c. stock or water
1 T. soy sauce or oyster sauce
1/4 t. salt, 1/2 t. sugar
1/8 t. pepper, 1 t. sesame oil
1 T. cornstarch

🦐　　🦐　　🦐

2 lbs. (900g) cangrejo, vivo en su carapacho
3 C. maicena

1/2 C. c/u, finamente picado: cebollín, raíz de jengibre, diente de ajo
1 1/2 C. frijoles negros fermentados, machacados

2 C. vino para cocinar
1 tz. caldo o agua
1 C. salsa de soya o salsa de ostiones
1/4 c. sal, 1/2 c. azúcar
1/8 c. pimienta, 1 c. aceite de sésamo
1 C. maicena

1 蟹處理乾淨，瀝乾切塊後約1斤(600公克)，蟹處理法見9頁，拌入太白粉備用。

2 油3大匙燒熱，將蟹兩面煎呈金黃色，略加油炒香 ❶ 料，再入調勻的 ❷ 料燒開後，蓋鍋續煮2分鐘(中途略炒拌)至蟹肉熟且汁呈濃狀即成。

桂花蟹　參考蔥薑炒蟹做法(見64頁)加炒好的香菇、洋蔥、筍及紅蘿蔔絲4兩(150公克)，再入打散的蛋3個炒至蛋剛凝固即成。

🦐　　🦐　　🦐

1 Prepare the crab (see p. 9); wash and drain. Cut into pieces. The crab after preparation should weigh 1 1/3 lbs. (600g). Coat with cornstarch.

2 Heat 3 T. oil. Pan-fry the crab until golden on both sides. Add a little oil; stir-fry **1** until fragrant; add mixture **2**; bring to boil; continue cooking, covered; stir during cooking, until crab is cooked through and the juice thickens, about 2 minutes.

Colorful Crab & Eggs Follow the same directions for making "Crab with Ginger & Onions" on p. 64. Add shredded and stir-fried black mushrooms, onions, bamboo, and carrot; total 1/3 lb. (150g). Then add 3 beaten eggs; stir-fry until the eggs are just set.

🦐　　🦐　　🦐

1 *Prepare el cangrejo (vea p. 9); lave y escurra. Corte en pedazos. Después de prepararse el cangrejo debe pesar 1 1/3 lbs. (600g). Reboce con maicena.*

2 *Caliente 3 C. de aceite. Sofría el cangrejo hasta que esté dorado por ambos lados. Agregue un poco de aceite; fría-revolviendo ❶ hasta que esté aromático; agregue la mezcla ❷ ; haga hervir; continúe cocinando, tapado; revuelva durante la cocción hasta que el cangrejo esté bien cocido y el líquido espese, como 2 minutos.*

Cangrejo y Huevos Pintorescos　*Siga las mismas instrucciones para hacer Cangrejo con Jengibre y Cebollas en p. 64. Agregue hongos negros en rebanadas ya sofritos, cebolla, bambú, y zanahoria; en total 1/3 lb. (150g). Luego agregue 3 huevos batidos; fría-revolviendo hasta que los huevos se cuajen.*

桂花蟹・Colorful Crab & Eggs
Cangrejo y Huevos Pintorescos

醋溜蟹　　　　　Sweet & Sour Crab

Cangrejo Agridulce

活蟹 ....1斤半(900公克)
太白粉 3大匙

①
糖、醋、水 各5大匙
番茄醬 5大匙
鹽 ....¼小匙
蒜末 ....½大匙
太白粉 1小匙

🦐　🦐　🦐

①
2 lbs. (900g) crab, live-in-shell
3 T. cornstarch

5 T. each: sugar, vinegar, water
5 T. ketchup
¼ t. salt
½ T. minced garlic cloves
1 t. cornstarch

🦐　🦐　🦐

①
2 lbs. (900g) cangrejo, vivo en su carapacho
3 C. maicena

5 C. c/u: azúcar, vinagre, agua
5 C. catsup
¹/₄ c. sal
¹/₂ C. diente de ajo finamente picado
1 c. maicena

1 蟹處理乾淨，瀝乾切塊後淨重約1斤(600公克)，蟹處理法見9頁；拌入太白粉備用。

2 油3大匙燒熱，將蟹塊煎至兩面呈金黃色約4分鐘(圖1)，隨即放入調勻的 **①** 料炒拌至汁成濃稠狀即成。

🦐　🦐　🦐

1 Prepare the crab (see p. 9); wash and drain; cut into pieces. The crab after preparation should weigh 1 1/3 lbs. (600g). Coat with cornstarch; set aside.

2 Heat 3 T. oil. Pan-fry the crab 4 minutes until golden on both sides (Fig. 1). Pour in mixture **①**; stir and cook until the liquid thickens; serve.

🦐　🦐　🦐

1 *Prepare el cangrejo (vea p. 9); lave y escurra; corte en pedazos. Después de prepararse el cangrejo debe pesar 1 1/3 lbs. (600g). Reboce con maicena; deje aparte.*

2 *Caliente 3 C. de aceite. Sofría el cangrejo hasta que esté dorado por ambos lados (Fig. 1). Vacíe la mezcla **①**; revuelva y cocine hasta que el líquido espese; sirva.*

1

乾燒蟹

Cangrejo Picante

Spicy Crab

2人份 · serves 2
2 porciones

活蟹 ....1斤半(900公克)
太白粉 1大匙

蔥末 2大匙
薑、蒜末 各1/2大匙
辣豆瓣醬 1小匙

酒釀*或酒 1大匙
番茄醬 4大匙
糖、太白粉 各1/2大匙
鹽 1/4小匙
高湯或水 3/4杯

≈ ≈ ≈

2 lbs. (900g) crab, live-in-shell
1 T. cornstarch

2 T. minced green onion
1/2 T. each, minced: ginger root, garlic cloves
1 t. chili bean paste

1 T. sweet brewed rice* or cooking wine
4 T. ketchup
1/2 T. each: sugar, cornstarch
1/4 t. salt
3/4 c. stock or water

≈ ≈ ≈

2 lbs. (900g) cangrejo, vivo en su carapacho
1 C. maicena

2 C. cebollín finamente picado
1/2 C. c/u, finamente picado: raíz de jengibre, diente de ajo
1 c. pasta de frijol picante

1 C. arroz dulce fermentado o vino para cocinar*
4 C. catsup
1/2 C. c/u: azúcar, maicena
1/4 c. sal
3/4 tz. caldo o agua

1 蟹處理乾淨，瀝乾切塊後淨重約1斤(600公克)，處理法見9頁。

2 油3大匙燒熱，將蟹煎至兩面呈金黃色，鏟於一邊，略加油炒香 **1** 料，再入調勻的 **2** 料連同鍋邊的蟹一起炒拌煮至汁呈濃稠狀即成。

＊ 酒釀是用糯米飯加糖發酵製成(見20頁，圖1)，市面上有現成的出售。

≈ ≈ ≈

1 Prepare crab (see p. 9); wash and drain; cut into pieces. The crab after preparation should weigh 1 1/3 lbs. (600g).

2 Heat 3 T. oil. Pan-fry crab until golden on both sides. Move to the side of the wok. Add a little oil; stir-fry **1** until fragrant; stir in mixture **2** ; spatula crab back to the center of wok; stir until combined and the juice thickens. Serve.

＊ Brewed rice is the fermentation of cooked glutinous rice and sugar (see p. 20, Fig. 1). Ready-made brewed rice is available in oriental markets.

≈ ≈ ≈

1 *Prepare el cangrejo (vea p. 9); lave y escurra; corte en pedazos. Después de prepararse el cangrejo debe pesar 1 1/3 lbs. (600g).*

2 *Caliente 3 C. de aceite. Sofría el cangrejo hasta que esté dorado por ambos lados. Muévalo hacia la orilla de la sartén wok. Agregue un poco de aceite; fría-revolviendo **1** hasta que esté aromático; agregue revolviendo la mezcla **2** ; use una espátula para regresar el cangrejo al centro de la sartén wok; revuelva hasta que se combine y el líquido espese. Sirva.*

＊ *Arroz fermentado es la fermentación de arroz glutinoso cocido y azúcar (vea p. 20, Fig. 1). Arroz fermentado ya preparado se encuentra en los mercados orientales.*

紅蟹米糕　Rice Pudding & Crab
Budín de Arroz y Cangrejo

活蟹 ....1斤半(900公克)
紅蔥頭(切片) 3大匙

① 瘦肉丁或瘦絞肉 1/2杯
香菇(泡軟、切丁) 1/4杯
蝦米(略泡水) 1/4杯

② 醬油 2大匙
酒、麻油 各1大匙
糖 1小匙
鹽 ......1/2小匙，胡椒 1/4小匙

長糯米 2杯

③ 水 11/2杯
醬油、油 各1大匙

2 lbs. (900g) crab, live-in-
  shell
3 T. sliced shallots

① 1/2 c. diced lean meat or
    ground lean meat
  1/4 c. presoftened Chinese
    black mushrooms, diced
  1/4 c. dried shrimp, soaked
    in water briefly

② 2 T. soy sauce
  1 T. each: cooking wine,
    sesame oil
  1 t. sugar
  1/2 t. salt, 1/4 t. pepper

2 c. long glutinous rice

③ 11/2 c. water
  1 T. each: soy sauce, oil

1 蟹處理乾淨，瀝乾切塊後淨重約1斤(600公克)，蟹處理法見9頁。

2 油4大匙燒至五分熱，入紅蔥頭炒至金黃色，隨入 ① 料炒香至肉變色，再加 ② 料炒勻備用。

3 糯米洗淨，加 ③ 料煮成飯，趁熱拌入炒好的材料，上置蟹大火蒸8分鐘即成。

1 Prepare crab (see p. 9); wash and drain; cut in pieces. The crab after preparation should weigh 1 1/3 lbs. (600g).

2 Heat 4 T. oil. Heat oil to medium. Stir-fry shallots until golden; add ①; stir-fry until fragrant and the meat changes color. Mix in ② until combined. Remove; set aside.

3 Rinse the rice. Mix ③ in rice; cook until done. Combine the cooked rice while hot with cooked mixture in step 2; top with crab; steam over high heat for 8 minutes; serve.

2 lbs. (900g) cangrejo, vivo en
  su carapacho
3 C. cebolla escalonia
  rebanada

① 1/2 tz. carne magra en cubitos o
    carne magra molida
  1/4 tz. hongos negros chinos
    ablandados, picados
  1/4 tz. camarón seco, remojado
    en agua brevemente

② 2 C. salsa de soya
  1 C. c/u: vino para cocinar,
    aceite de sésamo
  1 c. azúcar
  1/2 c. sal, 1/4 c. pimienta

2 tz. arroz glutinoso de grano
  largo

③ 11/2 tz. agua
  1 C. c/u: salsa de soya, aceite

1 Prepare el cangrejo (vea p. 9); lave y escurra; corte en pedazos. Después de prepararse el cangrejo debe pesar 1 1/3 lbs. (600g).

2 Caliente 4 C. de aceite. Caliente el aceite a fuego moderado. Fría-revolviendo la cebolla hasta que esté dorada; agregue ①; fría-revolviendo hasta que esté aromático y la carne cambie de color. Agregue mezclando ② hasta que se combine. Retire; deje aparte.

3 Enjuague el arroz. Mezcle ③ en el arroz; cocine hasta que se cueza. Combine el arroz cocido mientras esté caliente con la mezcla cocida del paso 2; cubra con el cangrejo; cocine al vapor a fuego alto por 8 minutos; sirva.

蟹塊粉絲煲 Crab & Bean Thread Casserole

Guiso de Cangrejo y Fideo

2人份・serves 2
2 porciones

中文材料

活蟹 ....1斤半(900公克)
麵粉 3大匙
粉絲 ....2把(100公克)
大白菜 ....6兩(225公克)

蒜末 1小匙
蔥(3公分長).....................6段
薑 6片
辣豆瓣醬或沙茶醬 1小匙

高湯 3杯
鹽、糖 各1/2小匙
醬油、酒、醋 各2小匙

English Ingredients

2 lbs. (900g) crab, live-in-
   shell
3 T. flour
2 pkg. vermicelli bean
   threads, 3.6 oz. (100g)
1/2 lb. (225g) napa cabbage

1 t. minced garlic cloves
6 sections green onion,
   1 1/4" (3cm) long
6 slices ginger root
1 t. chili bean paste or
   barbecue (sa-tsa) sauce

3 c. stock
1/2 t. each: salt, sugar
2 t. each: soy sauce,
   cooking wine, vinegar

Spanish Ingredients

2 lbs. (900g) cangrejo, vivo en
   su carapacho
3 C. harina
2 paquetes fideo vermicelli
   delgado, 3.6 oz (100g)
1/2 lb. (225g) repollo napa

1 c. diente de ajo finamente
   picado
6 secciones de cebollín,
   1 1/4"(3cm) de largo
6 rebanadas raíz de jengibre
1 c. pasta de frijol picante o
   salsa de barbacoa (sa-tsa)

3 tz. caldo
1/2 c. c/u: sal, azucar
2 c. c/u: salsa de soya, vino
   para cocinar, vinagre

中文做法

1 蟹處理乾淨，瀝乾切塊後淨重約1斤(600公克)，拌入麵粉，蟹處理法見9頁。粉絲泡軟、切段，白菜切塊、燙軟備用。

2 油3大匙燒熱，將蟹塊煎至兩面呈金黃色約4分鐘鏟出。

3 油2大匙燒熱，炒香 **1** 料加 **2** 料燒開，放入蟹塊、白菜及粉絲燒開蓋鍋中火續煮5分鐘即成。

English Method

1 Prepare crab (see p. 9); wash and drain, cut in pieces. The crab after preparation should weigh 1 1/3 lbs. (600g). Dredge with flour. Soak bean threads in cold water until softened. Cut in sections. Cut cabbage in pieces; cook in boiling water until tender. Set aside.

2 Heat 3 T. oil. Pan-fry the crab 4 minutes until golden on both sides; remove.

3 Heat 2 T. oil. Stir-fry **1** until fragrant; add **2**; bring to boil. Add crab, cabbage, then bean threads; bring to another boil; cover and cook over medium heat 5 minutes; serve.

Spanish Method

1 Prepare el cangrejo (vea p. 9); lave y escurra; corte en pedazos. Después de prepararse el cangrejo debe pesar 1 1/3 lbs. (600g). Reboce con harina. Remoje el fideo en agua fría hasta que se ablande. Corte en secciones. Corte el repollo en pedazos; cocine en agua hirviendo hasta que esté tierno. Deje aparte.

2 Caliente 3 C. de aceite. Sofría el cangrejo por 4 minutos hasta que esté dorado por ambos lados; retire.

3 Caliente 2 C. de aceite. Fría-revolviendo **1** hasta que esté aromático; agregue **2** ; haga hervir. Agregue el cangrejo, repollo, luego el fideo; hierva de nuevo; tape y cueza a fuego moderado por 5 minutos; sirva.

三杯蟹   Three Sauce Crab

Cangrejo en Tres Salsas

活蟹 ....1斤半(900公克)
太白粉 3大匙
麻油 3大匙

① 薑 10片
  蒜(拍破) 6瓣
  乾辣椒(切段) 1支

② 酒、水 各1/4杯
  醬油 1大匙
  糖 1/2大匙

蒜苗(切段) ....隨意

🦐   🦐   🦐

2 lbs. (900g) crab, live-in-shell
3 T. cornstarch
3 T. sesame oil

① **10 slices ginger root**
6 garlic cloves, mashed
1 dried hot pepper, cut in pieces

② **1/4 c. each: cooking wine, water**
1 T. soy sauce
1/2 T. sugar

fresh garlic pieces as desired

🦐   🦐   🦐

2 lbs. (900g) cangrejo, vivo en su carapacho
3 C. maicena
3 C. aceite de sésamo

① *10 rebanadas raíz de jengibre*
6 dientes de ajo, machacados
1 chile picante seco, picado

② *1/4 tz. c/u: vino para cocinar, agua*
1 C. salsa de soya
1/2 C. azúcar

ajo fresco al gusto

① 蟹處理乾淨，瀝乾切塊後淨重約1斤(600公克)，蟹處理法見9頁；拌入太白粉備用。

② 麻油3大匙燒熱，用中火將 ① 料炒香約2分鐘呈金黃色撈出，餘油入蟹煎至兩面呈金黃色約4分鐘，再加 ② 料及炒好的 ① 料燒開，翻拌至汁收乾，隨意撒上蒜苗即成。

🦐   🦐   🦐

① Prepare crab (see p. 9); wash and drain. Cut in pieces. The crab after preparation should weigh 1 1/3 lbs. (600g). Coat with cornstarch.

② Heat 3 T. sesame oil. Stir-fry ① over medium heat 2 minutes until golden; remove. With remaining oil in the wok, pan-fry crab until golden on both sides, about 4 minutes. Add ② and return ① to wok; bring to boil; stir and cook until the liquid has evaporated. Sprinkle with fresh garlic pieces if desired. Remove and serve.

🦐   🦐   🦐

① *Prepare el cangrejo (vea p. 9); lave y escurra; corte en pedazos. Después de prepararse el cangrejo debe pesar 1 1/3 lbs. (600g). Reboce con maicena.*

② *Caliente 3 C. de aceite de sésamo. Fría-revolviendo ① a fuego moderado hasta que esté dorado, 2 minutos; retire. Con el aceite restante en la sartén wok, sofría el cangrejo hasta que esté dorado por ambos lados, como por 4 minutos. Agregue ② y regrese ① a la sartén; haga hervir; revuelva y cueza hasta que el líquido se haya evaporado. Espolvoree con ajo fresco picado si lo desea. Saque y sirva.*

三杯小卷　Three Sauce Squid

Calamar en Tres Salsas

魷魚(小卷) ....6兩(225公克)
麻油 3大匙
粉絲 ....1把(50公克)

薑 10片
蒜(拍破) 6瓣
乾辣椒(切段) 1支

酒 1/2杯
高湯或水 1杯
醬油 2大匙
糖 2/3大匙

九層塔(無亦可) 1/2杯

🐟　🐟　🐟

1/2 lb. (225g) small squid
3 T. sesame oil
1 pkg. vermicelli bean
　　threads, 1.8oz (50g)

10 slices ginger root
6 garlic cloves, mashed
1 dried hot pepper, cut in
　　pieces

1/2 c. cooking wine
1 c. stock or water
2 T. soy sauce
2/3 T. sugar

1/2 c. fresh basil, optional

🐟　🐟　🐟

1/2 lb. (225g) calamar chico
3C. aceite de sésamo
1 paquete fideo vermicelli
　delgado, 1.8 oz. (50g)

10 rebanadas raíz de jengibre
6 dientes de ajo, machacados
1 chile picante seco, picado

1/2 tz. vino para cocinar
1 tz. caldo o agua
2 C. salsa de soya
2/3 C. azucar

1/2 tz. albahaca fresca,
　opcional

1 小卷抽出軟骨洗淨瀝乾，不去皮亦可；切環狀（鬚可食），粉絲泡軟切半。

2 麻油3大匙燒熱，用中火將 1 料炒香約2分鐘呈金黃色，隨入小卷爆出水份約2分鐘，續入 2 料燒開煮5分鐘至湯汁剩一半時，加入粉絲燒開至汁略收後，再加九層塔即成。

🐟　🐟　🐟

1 Pull out the long, transparent, sword-shaped cuttlebone from the squid. Wash and drain (with or without the membrane); cut the body into rings. Antennae on the squid's head are edible. Soak bean threads in cold water until softened; cut in half .

2 Heat 3 T. sesame oil. Stir-fry 1 over medium heat until fragrant or golden, about 2 minutes. Stir in squid and cook 2 minutes until water in squid is extracted. Pour in 2 ; bring to boil; cook 5 more minutes or until half the liquid is left. Add bean threads; return to boil; cook until liquid evaporates a little; add fresh basil. Remove and serve.

🐟　🐟　🐟

1 *Quítele el jibión largo, transparente, en forma de espada al calamar. Lave y escurra (con o sin la membrana);corte el cuerpo en anillos. Las antenas del calamar son comestibles. Remoje los fideos delgados en agua fría hasta que se ablanden; corte por la mitad.*

2 *Caliente 3 C. de aceite de sésamo. Fría-revolviendo 1 a fuego moderado hasta que esté aromático y dorado, como por 2 minutos. Agregue revolviendo el calamar y cocine por 2 minutos hasta que haya extraído el líquido. Vacíe 2 ; haga hervir; cocine por 5 minutos más o hasta que quede la mitad del líquido. Agregue el fideo; vuelva a hervir; cueza hasta que el líquido evapore un poco; agregue la albahaca fresca. Retire y sirva.*

時菜魷魚
Squid & Vegetables

魷魚或墨魚 ....1斤(600公克)

1
酒 ....¹/₂大匙
鹽 ....¹/₃小匙

2
蔥(3公分長) 6段
蒜(切片) 2瓣
辣椒(切段) 1支

3
香菇(泡軟切半) 3朵
大黃瓜或菜心(切塊燙熟) ...2杯
花菜或白蘿蔔(切塊燙熟) ...2杯

4
高湯 1¹/₂杯
醬油、黑醋 各1¹/₄大匙
糖、酒 ....各¹/₂大匙
鹽、麻油 ....各¹/₃小匙
太白粉 1¹/₂大匙

香菜 ....隨意

🐟　🐟　🐟

1¹/₃ lbs. (600g) squid or
　　cuttlefish

1
¹/₂ T. cooking wine
¹/₃ t. salt

2
6 sections green onion,
　　1¹/₄" (3cm) long
2 garlic cloves, sliced
1 hot pepper, cut in pieces

3
3 presoftened Chinese
　　black mushrooms, cut in
　　half
2 c. cucumber or vegetable
　　stalks, cut in pieces and
　　blanched
2 c. cauliflower or white
　　radish, cut in pieces and
　　blanched

4
1¹/₂ c. stock
1¹/₄ T. each: soy sauce,
　　black vinegar
¹/₂ T. each: sugar, cooking
　　wine
¹/₃ t. each: salt, sesame
　　oil
1¹/₂ T. cornstarch

coriander as desired

1 魷魚處理乾淨，拭乾水份後淨重約8兩(300公克)，在內面切交叉紋再切塊，魷魚處理法見9頁；拌入 **1** 料備用。

2 油2大匙燒熱，炒香 **2** 料，隨入 **3** 料略炒，續入調勻的 **4** 料及魷魚炒拌呈濃狀，再撒入香菜則味道更佳。

☐ 大黃瓜要去皮、去籽後再切塊，花菜分切小朵(圖1)。

🐟　🐟　🐟

1 Prepare squid; wash and pat dry (see p. 9). The squid after preparation should weigh 2/3 lb. (300g). Score the inside surface of the squid crosswise then cut the squid in pieces. Mix in **1**. Set aside.

2 Heat 2 T. oil; stir-fry **2** until fragrant; stir in **3** briefly; add mixture **4** and squid; stir and cook until the liquid thickens. Sprinkle coriander to add more flavor.

☐ Peel cucumber and remove seeds before cutting into pieces. Cut cauliflower into small flowerets (Fig. 1).

1

Calamar y Vegetales

Fotos a la izq.

4 porciones

¹/₃ lbs. (600g) calamar o jibia

2 C. vino para cocinar

3 c. sal

secciones de cebollín, 1¹/₄ " (3cm) de largo
dientes de ajo, rebanados
chile picante, picado

hongos negros chinos ablandados, cortados por la mitad
tz. pepino o tallos de vegetales, cortados en pedazos y sumergidos en agua hirviendo
tz. coliflor o rábano blanco, cortados en pedazos y sumergidos en agua hirviendo

¹/₂ tz. caldo, 1¹/₂ C. maicena
¹/₄ C. c/u: salsa de soya, vinagre negro
2 C. c/u: azúcar, vino para cocinar
3 c. c/u: sal, aceite de sésamo

cilantro al gusto

1 Prepare el calamar; lave y seque ligeramente (vea p. 9). Después de prepararse el calamar debe pesar 2/3 lb. (300g). Haga tajadas en la superficie interior del calamar en forma de equis luego córtelo en pedazos. Mezcle en **1**. Deje aparte.

2 Caliente 2 C. de aceite; fría-revolviendo **2** hasta que esté aromático; agregue revolviendo **3** brevemente; agregue la mezcla **4** y el calamar; revuelva y cocine hasta que el líquido espese. Espolvoréele el cilantro para darle más sabor.

☐ Pele el pepino y quítele las semillas antes de cortar en pedazos. Corte el coliflor en florecillas pequeñas (p. 76, Fig. 1).

蒜苔魷魚 / Calamar Sofrito — Stir-fried Squid

2人份 · serves 2

2 porciones

1 魷魚處理乾淨，拭乾後淨重約6兩(225公克)，切絲。蒜苔折去老莖切4公分長。

2 油2大匙燒熱，放入蒜苔略炒撈出。

3 油3大匙燒熱，入魷魚炒至變色，隨入蒜苔及 **1** 料炒拌均勻即成。

魷魚或墨魚 ....12兩(450公克)
蒜苔或韭菜花 .....6兩(225公克)
酒 1大匙
鹽、糖、麻油 ....各¹/₂小匙

lb. (450g) squid or cuttlefish
¹/₂ lb. (225g) chive buds

T. cooking wine
¹/₂ t. each: salt, sugar, sesame oil

1 Prepare squid; wash and pat dry. The squid after preparation should weigh 1/2 lb. (225g). Shred the squid. Discard the old stems from chive buds, then cut them into 1 1/4" (4cm) long sections.

2 Heat 2 T. oil; stir-fry chive buds briefly; remove.

3 Heat 3 T. oil. Stir-fry squid until color changes. Add **1** and return chive buds to wok; stir and cook until combined.

lb. (450g) calamar o jibia
¹/₂ lb. (225g) brotes de cebollín

C. vino para cocinar
¹/₂ c. c/u: sal, azúcar, aceite de sésamo

1 Prepare el calamar; lave y seque ligeramente. Después de prepararse el calamar debe pesar 1/2 lb. (225g). Desmenuce el calamar. Quítele y tire los tallos viejos de los brotes al cebollín, luego corte en secciones de 1 1/4" (4cm) de largo.

2 Caliente 2 C. de aceite; fría-revolviendo los brotes de cebollín brevemente; retire.

3 Caliente 3 C. de aceite. Fría-revolviendo el calamar hasta que cambie de color. Agregue **1** y regrese los brotes de cebollín a la sartén wok; revuelva y cocine hasta que esté mezclado.

魚香墨花
Jibia Picante

Spicy Cuttlefish

墨魚或魷魚 ....12兩(450公克)
辣豆瓣醬 1小匙

① 酒、太白粉 各1大匙
　 鹽 1/6小匙

② 蔥、薑、蒜末 各1大匙

③ 荸薺(切片)、木耳(泡軟、切片)、
　 豌豆莢 共2杯

④ 水 ....3大匙，醋 1/2大匙
　 醬油 11/2大匙
　 糖、麻油、太白粉 各1小匙

🐦　🐦　🐦

1 lb. (450g) cuttlefish or
　squid
1 t. chili bean paste

① 1 T. each: cooking wine,
　cornstarch
　1/6 t. salt

② 1 T. each, minced: green
　onion, ginger root, garlic
　cloves

③ 2 c. total: Chinese snow
　peas; water chestnuts
　& presoftened dried
　wood ears, both sliced

④ 3 T. water, 1/2 T. vinegar
　11/2 T. soy sauce
　1 t. each: sugar, sesame
　oil, cornstarch

🐦　🐦　🐦

1 lb. (450g) jibia o calamar
1 c. pasta de frijol picante

① *1 C. c/u: vino para cocinar,*
　maicena
　1/6 c. sal

② *1 C. c/u, finamente picado:*
　cebollín, raíz de jengibre,
　diente de ajo

③ *2 tz. en total: chícharos chinos,*
　castañas en agua rebanadas
　y orejas de madera
　ablandadas, rebanadas

④ *3 C. agua, 1/2 C. vinagre*
　11/2 C. salsa de soya
　1 c. c/u: azúcar, aceite de
　sésamo, maicena

1 墨魚處理乾淨，拭乾水份切塊(見9頁)，淨重約6兩(225公克)，亦可先切條後斜切花紋，轉方向一邊交叉切一邊切塊(圖1)，拌入 ① 料備用。

2 油2大匙燒熱，入 ③ 料略炒(如太乾加水1大匙)撈出。

3 油2大匙燒熱，炒香 ② 料及辣豆瓣醬，隨入墨魚炒至捲起，再加調勻的 ④ 料及炒好的 ③ 料炒拌均勻即可。

🐦　🐦　🐦

1 Prepare the cuttlefish (see p. 9); wash and pat dry; cut in pieces. The cuttlefish after preparation should weigh 1/2 lb. (225g). Or, cut cuttlefish in strips then make diagonal cuts; turn cuttlefish and make diagonal cuts from opposite direction to form crisscross cuts, then cut into pieces (Fig. 1). Marinate in ① ; set aside.

2 Heat 2 T. oil. Stir in ③ briefly (add water if too dry); remove.

3 Heat 2 T. oil. Stir-fry ② and chili bean paste until fragrant; stir in cuttlefish until curled. Add mixture ④ ; return ③ to wok; mix well. Serve.

🐦　🐦　🐦

1 *Prepare la jibia (vea p. 9); lave y seque ligeramente; corte en pedazos. Después de prepararse la jibia debe pesar 1/2 lb. (225g). O, corte la jibia en tiritas luego hágale tajadas diagonales; voltee la jibia y hágale cortes diagonales en dirección contraria para formar tajadas en forma de equis, luego corte en pedazos (Fig. 1). Marine en ① ; deje aparte.*

2 *Caliente 2 C. de aceite. Agregue ③ revolviendo brevemente (agregue agua si está muy seco); retire.*

3 *Caliente 2 C. de aceite. Fría-revolviendo ② y la pasta de frijol picante hasta que esté aromático; agregue revolviendo la jibia hasta que se enrosque. Agregue la mezcla ④ ; regrese ③ a la sartén wok; mezcle bien. Sirva.*

1

蘆筍魷魚　　Squid & Asparagus
Calamar y Espárragos

2人份・serves 2
2 porciones

魷魚或墨魚 ....12兩(450公克)
酒、太白粉 各1大匙
鹽 1/6小匙

蔥、薑、蒜末 各1大匙

蘆筍(切段)，筍、洋菇(切片)共2杯

水 ....3大匙，太白粉 1小匙
鹽、糖、麻油 各1/3小匙

🍃　🍃　🍃

1 lb. (450g) squid or cuttlefish

1 T. each: cooking wine, cornstarch
1/6 t. salt

1 T. each, minced: green onion, ginger root, garlic cloves

2 c. total: sectioned asparagus, sliced bamboo shoots, and mushrooms

3 T. water, 1 t. cornstarch
1/3 t. each: salt, sugar, sesame oil

🍃　🍃　🍃

1 lb. (450g) calamar o jibia

1 C. c/u: vino para cocinar, maicena
1/6 c. sal

1 C. c/u, finamente picado: cebollín, raíz de jengibre, diente de ajo

2 tz. en total: espárragos cortados en secciones, brotes de bambú en rebanadas, y hongos

3 C. agua, 1 c. maicena
1/3 c. c/u: sal, azúcar, aceite de sésamo

1 將魷魚處理乾淨，拭乾水份後淨重約6兩(225公克)，在內面切交叉紋再切塊，魷魚處理法見9頁；拌入 **1** 料備用。

2 油2大匙燒熱，入 **3** 料略炒(如太乾加水1大匙)撈出。

3 油2大匙炒香 **2** 料，隨入魷魚炒至捲起，再加 **4** 料及 **3** 料炒拌均勻即可。

西芹魷魚 將 **3** 料改用芹菜2杯，其他材料及作法同上。

🍃　🍃　🍃

1 Prepare squid; wash and pat dry. The squid after preparation should weigh 1/2 lb. (225g). Make crisscross cuts diagonally on the inside surface of the squid, then cut in pieces (see p. 9). Mix in **1**; set aside.

2 Heat 2 T. oil. Stir-fry **3** briefly (add a little water if too dry); remove.

3 Heat 2 T. oil. Stir-fry **2** until fragrant. Stir in squid until curled. Add **4** and return **3** to wok; stir and cook until combined; serve.

Squid & Celery Use 2 c. sliced celery for ingredients **3**. Other ingredients and procedures are the same as above .

🍃　🍃　🍃

1 *Prepare el calamar; lave y seque ligeramente. Después de la preparación el calamar debe pesar 1/2 lb. (225g). Haga cortes diagonales en forma de equis en la superficie interior del calamar, luego corte en pedazos (vea p. 9). Mezcle en* **1***; deje aparte.*

2 *Caliente 2 C. de aceite. Fría-revolviendo* **3** *brevemente (agregue un poco de agua si está muy seco); retire.*

3 *Caliente 2 C. de aceite. Fría-revolviendo* **2** *hasta que esté aromático. Agregue revolviendo el calamar hasta que se enrosque. Agregue* **4** *y regrese* **3** *a la sartén wok; revuelva y cocine hasta que esté mezclado; sirva.*

Calamar y Apio *Use 2 tz. de apio rebanado para los ingredientes en* **3**. *Los otros ingredientes y procedimientos son como arriba.*

西芹魷魚・Squid & Celery
Calamar y Apio

五味魷魚　　Five Flavored Squid

Calamar de Cinco Sabores

2人份・serves 2
2 porciones

新鮮魷魚或已發泡的乾魷魚
　(圖1)................1斤(600公克)

① 番茄醬 2大匙
醬油、黑醋 各1大匙
糖 1/2大匙
蔥、薑、蒜、辣椒末.....各1小匙

🥄　🥄　🥄

1 1/3 lbs. (600g) fresh
　squid or presoftened
　dried squid (Fig. 1)

① 2 T. ketchup
1 T. each: soy sauce, black
　vinegar
1/2 T. sugar
1 t. each, minced: green
　onion, ginger root, garlic
　cloves, chili pepper

🥄　🥄　🥄

*1 1/3 lbs. (600g) calamar
　fresco o calamar seco
　ablandado (Fig. 1)*

① *2 C. catsup
1 C. c/u: salsa de soya, vinagre
　negro
1/2 C. azúcar
1 c. c/u, finamente picado:
　cebollín, raíz de jengibre,
　diente de ajo, chile*

1 魷魚處理乾淨，拭乾水份後淨重約半斤(300公克)，在內面切交叉紋再切塊，魷魚處理法見9頁；將 ① 料調勻即為調味汁。

2 水燒開，入魷魚川燙1分鐘至捲起剛熟即撈出，淋或沾調味汁食用。

🥄　🥄　🥄

1 Prepare squid; wash and pat dry. The squid after preparation should weigh 2/3 lb. (300g). Make crisscross cuts diagonally on the inside surface then cut in pieces (see p. 9). Stir ① thoroughly into sauce.

2 Bring water to boil; plunge squid in boiling water 1 minute; remove quickly when curled. Sprinkle sauce over squid; serve. Or, serve the sauce as a dip with squid.

🥄　🥄　🥄

1 *Prepare el calamar; lave y seque ligeramente. Después de la preparación el calamar debe pesar 2/3 lb. (300g). Haga cortes diagonales en forma de equis en la superficie interior del calamar, luego corte en pedazos (vea p. 9). Mezcle ① completamente formando una salsa.*

2 *Hierva agua; sumerja el calamar en el agua hirviendo por 1 minuto; saque rápidamente cuando se enrosque. Vacíe la salsa sobre el calamar; sirva. O, sirva la salsa como un dip para el calamar.*

1

薑汁魷魚　Squid in Ginger Sauce

Calamar en Salsa de Jengibre

新鮮魷魚或已發泡的乾魷魚.......
..................1斤(600公克)

醬油 3大匙
醋 ......1½大匙，糖 ....½大匙
麻油 1大匙
薑、蒜、辣椒末...........各1小匙

❧　❧　❧

1⅓ lbs. (600g) fresh
　squid or presoftened
　fried squid

3 T. soy sauce
1½ T. vinegar, ½ T. sugar
1 T. sesame oil
1 t. each, minced: ginger
　root, garlic cloves, chili
　pepper

❧　❧　❧

*1⅓ lbs. (600g) calamar fresco
　o calamar seco ablandado*

*3 C. salsa de soya
1½ C. vinagre, ½ C. azúcar
1 C. aceite de sésamo
1 c. c/u, finamente picado: raíz
　de jengibre, diente de ajo,
　chile*

1　魷魚處理乾淨，拭乾水份後淨重約半斤(300公克)，在內面切交叉紋再切塊，魷魚處理法見9頁；將 ❶ 料調勻即為調味汁。

2　水燒開，入魷魚川燙1分鐘至捲起剛熟即撈出，淋或沾調味汁食用。

❧　❧　❧

1　Prepare squid; wash and pat dry. The squid after preparation should weigh 2/3 lb. (300g).　Score crisscross cuts diagonally on the inside surface.　Then cut into pieces (see p. 9). Stir ❶ thoroughly into sauce.

2　Bring water to boil; plunge squid in boiling water 1 minute; remove quickly when curled.　Sprinkle sauce over squid; serve.　Or, serve the sauce as a dip with squid.

❧　❧　❧

1　*Prepare el calamar; lave y seque ligeramente. Después de la preparación el calamar debe pesar 2/3 lb. (300g). Haga cortes diagonales en forma de equis en la superficie interior del calamar, luego corte en pedazos (vea p. 9). Mezcle ❶ completamente formando una salsa.*

2　*Hierva agua; sumerja el calamar en el agua hirviendo por 1 minuto; saque rápidamente cuando se enrosque. Vacíe la salsa sobre el calamar; sirva. O, sirva la salsa como un dip para el calamar.*

Camarones al Horno

蝦18條.............半斤(300公克)
酒.................................1大匙
鐵簽或竹簽 18支
檸檬..............................½個
① 鹽.............................½小匙胡
椒、辣椒粉 ....各⅛小匙

🦐   🦐   🦐

18 shrimp, ⅔ lb. (300g)
1 T. cooking wine
18 wooden or steel
   skewers
½ lemon

½ t. salt
① ⅛ t. each: black pepper,
chili pepper

🦐   🦐   🦐

18 camarones, ⅔ lb. (300g)
1 C. vino para cocinar
18 palillos de madera o hierro
   para brochetas
½ limón

½ c. sal
① ⅛ c. c/u: pimienta negra,
   chile

① 蝦用竹簽串上，兩面塗上酒使表面略濕，再均勻撒上 ① 料備用。

② 烤箱燒至550˚F(290˚C)，將蝦置中層烤5分鐘，再翻面烤5分鐘至有香味肉剛
熟即取出(若烤過熟肉粗無汁)，食時淋適量檸檬汁即可。

☐ 串蝦可使用橫串(圖1)，適於在炭火上烤，整片烤後把竹簽抽出即可。也可直
串，串入時由尾部經過腹部將蝦串直，以免烤後彎曲。

🦐   🦐   🦐

① Thread a skewer through each shrimp. Moisten each shrimp with wine.
Sprinkle ① on shrimp evenly. Set aside.

② Preheat oven to 550˚F (290˚C). Bake the shrimp on a middle rack of
the oven for 5 minutes. Turn them over; bake another 5 minutes until
fragrant and cooked; remove quickly. (If over-baked, the meat will be too
tough and not juicy.) Sprinkle on lemon juice before serving.

☐ Horizontally-skewered shrimp (Fig. 1) are suited to grilling over hot
coals. After the shrimp are done, remove the skewers and serve. Vertically
skewered shrimp are threaded from tail to belly to prevent curling during
baking.

🦐   🦐   🦐

① *Inserte un palillo en cada camarón. Rocíe cada camarón con vino.
Espolvoree ① en los camarones por parejo. Deje aparte.*

② *Precaliente el horno a 550ºF (290ºC). Hornee los camarones en la
parrilla central por 5 minutos. Voltéelos; hornee por 5 minutos más hasta
que estén aromáticos; saque rápidamente. (Si se cocina demasiado, la
carne estará muy dura y no jugosa.) Rocíele el jugo de limón antes de
servir.*

☐ *Camarones insertados horizontalmente (Fig. 1) son apropiados para la
parrilla sobre brasas calientes. Después que estén cocidos, quítelos de los
palillos y sirva. Camarones insertados verticalmente se insertan desde la
cola hasta el estómago para que no se enrosquen al hornear.*

1

烤魷魚
Calamar al Horno

Baked Squid

2人份・serves 2
2 porciones

魷魚 ....1斤(600公克)
酒 1大匙

鹽 ....¼小匙
胡椒、辣椒粉 ....各¹⁄₁₆小匙

黑或白芝麻 1小匙
檸檬 ....½個
椒鹽 ....適量

🐟　🐟　🐟

1⅓ lbs. (600g) squid
1 T. cooking wine

¼ t. salt
¹⁄₁₆ t. each: black pepper,
　chili pepper

1 t. black or white sesame
　seeds
½ lemon
Szechuan peppercorn salt
　as desired

🐟　🐟　🐟

1⅓ lbs. (600g) calamar
1 C. vino para cocinar

¼ c. sal
¹⁄₁₆ c. c/u: pimienta negra, chile

1 c. semillas de sésamo negras
　o blancas
½ limón
sal de grano de pimienta al
　gusto

1 魷魚處理乾淨，拭乾水份後淨重約半斤(300公克)，在内面切交叉紋，魷魚處理法見9頁；兩面塗上酒使表面略濕，再均匀撒上 **1** 料及芝麻。

2 烤箱燒至550°F(290°C)，將魷魚置中層烤10分鐘至中間部份略膨脹肉熟即取出切塊置盤，淋入適量的檸檬汁或沾椒鹽食用。

海鮮大拼　烤魷魚可與多樣海鮮搭配成海鮮大拼。

🐟　🐟　🐟

1 Prepare squid; wash and pat dry. The squid after preparation should weigh 2/3 lb. (300g). Make crisscross cuts on the inside surface of the squid (see p. 9). Brush squid with wine on both sides to moisten; sprinkle **1** and sesame evenly over squid.

2 Preheat oven to 550°F (290°C). Bake squid 10 minutes on the middle rack until cooked and center part has expanded a little. Remove and cut in pieces; arrange on a plate. Sprinkle with lemon juice; serve. Or serve with Szechuan peppercorn salt as a dip.

Assorted Seafood Platter　This dish may be accompanied by, and arranged with, various seafoods to create an Assorted Seafood Platter.

🐟　🐟　🐟

1 *Prepare el calamar; lave y seque ligeramente. Después de la preparación el calamar debe pesar 2/3 lb. (300g). Haga cortes diagonales en forma de equis en la superficie interior del calamar (vea p. 9). Cepille el calamar con vino por ambos lados para humedecer; espolvoree **1** y el sésamo en el calamar por parejo.*

2 *Precaliente el horno a 550ºF (290ºC). Hornee el calamar por 10 minutos en la parrilla central hasta que esté cocido y la parte central se expanda un poco. Saque y corte en pedazos; coloque en un plato. Rocíele el jugo de limón; sirva. O sirva con sal de grano de pimienta szechuan como dip.*

Plato de Mariscos Surtidos　*Este platillo puede ser complementado y arreglado con varias clases de mariscos para hacer un Plato de Mariscos Surtidos .*

海鮮大拼・Assorted Seafood Platter
Plato de Mariscos Surtidos

海鮮蒸蛋　Steamed Eggs & Seafood

Huevos al Vapor con Mariscos　宴客菜・Serve at formal meal
Se sirve en una cena formal

①
蟹(切塊) 1隻
蛤蜊、蝦仁 各6隻
鮑魚、海參 各6塊
生蠔 ....3兩(115公克)

蛋(大) 3個

②
酒 1大匙
鹽、麻油 各1小匙
高湯 3杯

③
鹽 ....¼小匙，高湯 2杯
太白粉 1⅓大匙

蔥花 2大匙

🐟　🐟　🐟

①
1 crab, cut into pieces
6 each: clams, shelled
　shrimp
6 pieces each: abalone,
　sea cucumber
¼ lb. (115g) oysters

3 large eggs

②
1 T. cooking wine
1 t. each: salt, sesame oil
3 c. stock

③
¼ t. salt, 2 c. stock
1⅓ T. cornstarch

2 T. chopped green onions

🐟　🐟　🐟

①
1 cangrejo, cortado en
　pedazos
6 c/u: almejas, camarones
　pelados
6 piezas c/u: abulón, pepino de
　mar
¼ lb. (115g) ostiones

3 huevos grandes

②
1 C. vino para cocinar
1 c. c/u: sal, aceite de sésamo
3 tz. caldo

③
¼ c. sal, 2 tz. caldo
1⅓ C. maicena

2 C. cebollín picado

家常蒸蛋・Home Style Steamed Eggs
Huevos al Vapor Estilo Casero

---

1 將 **①** 料處理好放入深盤內，蛋打散拌入 **②** 料也倒入深盤內；水燒開小火蒸20分鐘(蒸時一定用小火；如用電鍋可打開一小縫)，熄火後再燜5分鐘即可。

2 將 **③** 料攪拌至燒開成薄糊狀，淋在蒸好的蛋上，撒上蔥花即成。

家常蒸蛋 蛋3個與 **②** 料攪勻，內可加魚糕、火腿、蛤蜊、芹菜、香菜、香菇或蒜頭等，水開小火蒸20分鐘即可。

🐟　🐟　🐟

1 Prepare all ingredients in **①** then place in a bowl. Beat the eggs and mix in **②** ; pour the egg mixture in the same bowl. Steam over boiling water and low heat (low heat is a must for successful steaming), 20 minutes. If a rice cooker is used, steam with cover cracked open a little until done. Unplug the cooker; let stand 5 minutes while covered. Remove.

2 Bring **③** to boil; stir until thin paste is formed. Pour over steamed eggs. Sprinkle with chopped green onions. Serve.

Home Style Steamed Eggs Beat 3 eggs and mix **②** in well. Fish cake, ham, clams, celery, coriander, black mushrooms, or garlic may be added, as desired. Steam over boiling water and low heat for 20 minutes; serve.

🐟　🐟　🐟

1 *Prepare todos los ingredientes de* **①** *luego coloque en un tazón. Bata los huevos y mezcle en* **②** *; vacíele la mezcla de huevos al tazón. Cocine al vapor sobre agua hirviendo y a fuego bajo (fuego bajo es necesario para obtener el mejor resultado cociendo al vapor), por 20 minutos. Si usa una olla para cocer arroz al vapor, cueza al vapor con la tapadera un poco destapada hasta que esté listo. Desconecte la olla, deje reposar por 5 minutos sin destapar. Retire.*

2 *Haga hervir* **③** *; revuelva hasta que se forme una pasta delgada. Vacíe sobre los huevos al vapor. Espolvoree con cebollín picado. Sirva.*

Huevos al Vapor Estilo Casero *Bata 3 huevos y mézclele* **②** *completamente. Se le puede agregar torta de pescado, jamón, almejas, apio, cilantro, hongos negros, o ajo al gusto. Cueza sobre agua hirviendo y a fuego bajo por 20 minutos; sirva.*

鮑魚蒸蛋　Steamed Eggs & Abalone

Huevos al Vapor con Abulón

宴客菜・Serve at formal meal
Se sirve en una cena formal

鮑魚或中蝦(由背部片開) ..12片
蝦漿或魚漿 ....4兩(150公克)
生鹹蛋黃或生鴿蛋 3個
香菇(泡軟、切條) 24條
蛋(大) 3個

酒 1大匙
鹽、麻油 各1小匙
高湯 3½杯

鹽 ....¼小匙
高湯 2杯
太白粉 1⅓大匙

🍃　🍃　🍃

**12 slices abalone or
medium shrimp (cut in
back and opened)**
**⅓ lb. (150g) shrimp paste
or fish cake**
**3 salty egg yolks or pigeon
eggs**
**24 presoftened Chinese
black mushroom shreds**
3 large eggs

1 T. cooking wine
1 t. each: salt, sesame oil
3½ c. stock

¼ t. salt
2 c. stock
1⅓ T. cornstarch

🍃　🍃　🍃

*12 rebanadas de abulón o
camarones medianos
(cortados por el dorso y
abiertos)*
*⅓ lb. (150g) pasta de camarón
o torta de pescado*
*3 yemas de huevo saladas o
huevos de pichón*
*24 rebanadas de hongos negros
chinos ablandados*
3 huevos grandes

1 C. vino para cocinar
*1 c. c/u: sal aceite de
sésamo*
3½ tz. caldo

¼ c. sal
2 tz. caldo
1⅓ C. maicena

1 蝦漿分成12份。鹹蛋黃每個切4，搓成小丸子。

2 鮑魚片撒少許太白粉，抹上蝦漿做凹狀，放入鹹蛋黃，兩邊各置一條香菇做成鳳眼狀，共做12份。

3 蛋打散拌入 ❶ 料，倒入深盤內，水燒開小火蒸12分鐘至蛋半凝固時，排入鳳眼鮑魚續用小火蒸8分鐘取出，將 ❷ 料攪拌至燒開淋在蛋上即成。

🍃　🍃　🍃

1 Divide shrimp paste into 12 porciones. Cut each salty egg yolk in quarters; roll into balls.

2 Sprinkle cornstarch over each abalone slice. Spread a portion of shrimp paste on top of abalone. Press an indentation in center of shrimp paste. Put in a salty egg ball. Arrange two strips of black mushroom on two sides of the egg ball to form a Phoenix eye. Follow the same procedure to make 11 more.

3 Beat eggs and mix in ❶ . Pour the egg mixture in a bowl, steam 12 minutes, over boiling water, using low heat until the egg mixture is half set. Arrange the abalone on top of the egg mixture in the bowl, continue steaming over low heat for another 8 minutes; remove. Stir and bring ❷ to a boil; remove and spread ❷ on the egg mixture; serve.

🍃　🍃　🍃

1 *Divida la pasta de camarón en 12 porciones. Corte cada yema salada en cuatro; enrolle formando bolitas.*

2 *Espolvoree maicena sobre cada rebanada de abulón. Haga una depresión en el centro de la pasta de camarón. Colóquele una bola de huevo. Acomode dos rebanadas de hongo negro en dos lados de la bola de huevo para formar un ojo Fénix. Siga el mismo procedimiento para preparar 11 más.*

3 *Bata los huevos y mezcle en ❶ . Ponga la mezcla de huevo en un tazón, cueza al vapor por 12 minutos, sobre agua hirviendo, a fuego bajo hasta que la mezcla de huevo esté medio cuajada. Acomode el abulón sobre la mezcla de huevo en el tazón, continúe cocinando al vapor a fuego bajo por otros 8 minutos; retire. Mezcle y haga hervir ❷ ; retire y unte ❷ sobre la mezcla de huevo; sirva.*

海產火鍋　Seafood Hot Pot (Huo Kuo)

Olla Caliente de Mariscos (Huo Kuo)

4人份・serves 4
4 porciones

① 蟹(切塊) 1隻
海參、魷魚、魚肉、魚糕.........各6片
蝦、蛤蜊 各6隻

② 大白菜(切塊) ....半斤(300公克)
番茄(切塊) 1個
鹹菜或榨菜 1/4杯，薑 2片

③ 高湯 ....6杯，酒 2大匙
鹽.........1¹/₂小匙，麻油、胡椒 各少許

④ 醬油 3大匙
薑末 ....1大匙，辣椒末 1小匙

❧　❧　❧

① 1 crab, cut in pieces
6 slices each: sea cucumber,
squid, fillet, steamed fish
cake(kamaboko)
6 each: shrimp, clams

② ²/3 lb. (300g) nappa cabbage,
cut into pieces
1 tomato, cut in pieces
1/4 c. pickled mustard cabbage
or Szechuan pickled
mustard greens
2 slices ginger root

③ 6 c. stock, 1¹/2 t. salt
2 T. cooking wine
sesame oil and pepper as
desired

④ 3 T. soy sauce
1 T. minced ginger root
1 t. minced chili pepper

❧　❧　❧

① *1 cangrejo, cortado en pedazos*
6 rebanadas c/u: pepino de mar,
calamar, filete, torta de
pescado al vapor (kamaboko)
6 c/u: camarones, almejas

② *²/3 lb. (300g) repollo napa, cortado*
en pedazos
1 tomate, cortado en pedazos
1/4 tz. repollo mostaza escabechado
o repollo "mustard greens"
Szechuan escabechado
2 rebanadas raíz de jengibre

③ *6 tz. caldo, 1¹/2 c. sal*
2 C. vino para cocinar
aceite de sésamo y pimienta al gusto

④ *3 C. salsa de soya*
1 C. raíz de jengibre finamente
picada
1 c. chile finamente picado

1

1 將 **②** 料放入 **③** 料內燒開，再加 **①** 料蓋鍋燒開，見蛤蜊殼開，其他海鮮均熟即可上桌沾 **④** 料食用。

2 或 **②** 料放入 **③** 料內燒開，將備好的 **①** 料邊煮邊食並沾 **④** 料食用。

□　火鍋內材料(圖1)可隨喜好任意選用，魚丸、蝦丸、香菇、唐好菜、菠菜、荷蘭豆、粉絲、牛或豬肉等均可。

❧　❧　❧

1 Combine **②** and **③** ; bring to boil; add **①** ; cover and cook until the clams are open and other ingredients are cooked; remove. Serve with **④** as a dip.

2 Or combine **②** and **③** ; bring to boil. Add **①** and cook while eating. Serve with **④** as a dip. This is a Chinese style cook-at-table dish (Fondue style). Continue to cook while serving and eating.

□　Fish balls, shrimp balls, black mushrooms, garlic, chrysanthemum, spinach, snow peas, vermicelli bean threads, beef, or pork (see Fig. 1 for ingredients) may be used for hot pot as desired.

❧　❧　❧

1 *Combine* **②** *y* **③** *; haga hervir; agregue* **①** *; tape y cocine hasta que se abran las almejas y los demás ingredientes se cuezan; retire. Sirva con* **④** *como dip.*

2 *O combine* **②** *y* **③** *; haga hervir. Agregue* **①** *y cocine mientras come. Sirva con* **④** *como dip. Este es un platillo estilo chino que se cocina en la mesa (estilo fondue). Continúe cocinando mientras sirve y come.*

□　*Puede usar bolas de pescado, bolas de camarón, hongos negros, ajo, crisantemo, espinaca, chícharos chinos, fideo delgado vermicelli, carne de res, o cerdo (vea Fig. 1 para ingredientes), al gusto, para la olla caliente.*

海鮮鍋飯
Arroz y Mariscos

米 3杯

乾魷魚(中) 1條
蝦 ..12隻，生蠔 ...4兩(150公克)
瘦肉或火腿(切丁) 1/2杯
蝦米(略洗) 2大匙

紅蘿蔔丁、洋菇丁、筍丁、
　　青豆仁 共2杯

水 ....3杯，胡椒 1/8小匙
醬油、酒 各2大匙
麻油 1/2大匙
鹽、糖 各1/2小匙

❧　❧　❧

3 c. rice

1 dried, medium squid
12 shrimp
1/3 lb. (150g) oysters
1/2 c. lean pork or ham,
　diced
2 T. dried shrimp, rinsed

2 c. total: green peas, diced
　carrots, mushrooms,
　bamboo shoots

3 c. water, 1/8 t. pepper
2 T. each: soy sauce, cooking
　wine
1/2 T. sesame oil
1/2 t. each: salt, sugar

❧　❧　❧

3 tz. arroz

1 calamar mediano, seco
12 camarones
1/3 lb. (150g) ostiones
1/2 tz. cerdo o jamón magro,
　picado en cubitos
2 C. camarón seco, lavado

2 tz. en total: chícharos,
　zanahoria picada en
　cubitos, hongos, brotes de
　bambú

3 tz. agua, 1/8 c. pimienta
2 C. c/u: salsa de soya, vino
　para cocinar
1/2 C. aceite de sésamo
1/2 c. c/u: sal, azúcar

① 米洗淨瀝乾，乾魷魚切小片，蝦去腸泥，生蠔大的略切備用。

② 將米及 ①、②、③ 料全部拌勻放入電鍋內(圖1)煮成飯，趁熱食用。

③ 如無電鍋可將全部材料拌勻放入普通深鍋內大火燒開1分鐘，攪拌蓋鍋改小火續煮20分鐘熄火，再燜10分鐘即可食用。

☐ 材料可隨喜好任意選用，干貝、乾鮑魚、蟹、海參、蛤蜊、鮮魷魚等。

❧　❧　❧

1 Rinse rice and drain. Cut squid in small pieces. Devein shrimp. Halve the big oysters. Set aside.

2 Combine rice with ①, ②, and ③; mix well. Cook the rice mixture in a rice cooker (Fig. 1). Serve hot.

3 A pot may substitute for a rice cooker. Bring rice mixture to a boil in pot; stir and cook for 1 minute. Reduce heat to low; cover and cook for another 20 minutes. Turn off heat; keep the pot covered for 10 more minutes; serve.

☐ Scallops, dry abalone, crab, sea cucumber, clams, and/or fresh squid etc. may be used, as desired, for this recipe.

❧　❧　❧

1 *Enjuague el arroz y escurra. Corte el calamar en pedazos pequeños. Desvene los camarones. Corte los ostiones por la mitad. Deje aparte.*

2 *Combine el arroz con ①, ②, y ③; mezcle bien. Cocine la mezcla de arroz en una olla para cocer arroz al vapor (Fig. 1). Sirva caliente.*

3 *Se puede usar una olla cualquiera por la olla para cocer arroz. Haga hervir la mezcla de arroz en una olla: revuelva y cocine por 1 minuto. Reduzca el fuego a bajo; tape y cocine por otros 20 minutos. Apague el fuego; mantenga la olla tapada por 10 minutos más; sirva.*

☐ *Puede usar escalopes, abulón seco, cangrejo, pepino de mar, almejas, y/o calamar fresco etc. al gusto, para esta receta.*

1

海鮮粥　Seafood Congee

Congee de Mariscos

蟹(小) 1隻
魚肉、生蠔 ......各4兩(150公克)
蛤蜊 8個
蝦(中) 12隻

高湯 6杯
飯 3杯
酒 2大匙
鹽 1¼小匙
胡椒 ....少許

芹菜或蔥(切粒) 2大匙
香菜 2大匙

🍵　🍵　🍵

1 small crab
¹/₃ lb. (150g) each: oysters,
**   fish fillet**
8 clams
12 medium shrimp

6 c. stock
3 c. hot cooked rice
2 T. cooking wine
1¼ t. salt
dash of pepper

2 T. celery or green onion,
**   chopped**
2 T. coriander

🍵　🍵　🍵

1 cangrejo pequeño
¹/₃ lb. (150g) c/u: ostiones,
*   filete de pescado*
8 almejas
12 camarones medianos

6 tz. caldo
3 tz. arroz cocido caliente
2 C. vino para cocinar
1¹/₄ c. sal
pizca de pimienta

2 C. apio o cebollín, picado
2 C. cilantro

1 將蟹、魚肉切塊，生蠔、蛤蜊加少許鹽輕抓洗淨，蝦去殼留尾備用。

2 將 **2** 料燒開後，放入 **1** 料再燒開，續煮4分鐘，食時撒上 **3** 料，隨意加少許麻油，可與饅頭或麵餅配食。

☐ 可將 **1** 料內的材料隨意取換搭配。

🍵　🍵　🍵

1 Cut crab and fish into pieces. Rub a little salt on oysters and clams then rinse. Shell shrimp but leave tails intact.

2 Bring **2** to a boil. Add **1** and return to boil; continue cooking for 4 minutes. Sprinkle **3** on top. Sesame oil may be added as desired. Serve with bun or tortilla.

☐ Ingredients in **1** may be changed as desired.

🍵　🍵　🍵

1 *Corte el cangrejo y el pescado en pedazos. Unte un poco de sal en los ostiones y almejas luego enjuague. Pele los camarones pero deje la cola intacta.*

2 *Haga hervir **2**. Agregue **1** y vuelva a hervir; continúe cocinando por 4 minutos. Espolvoréele **3** encima. Puede agregar aceite de sésamo al gusto. Sirva con pan o tortillas.*

☐ *Los ingredientes de **1** se pueden substituir al gusto suyo.*

海鮮玉米湯   **Seafood Corn Soup**

Sopa de Mariscos con Elote

蝦仁(中) 12隻
鮮干貝(或魚肉) 3個
大蜆 8個

玉米罐頭 1罐
高湯或水 5杯
酒 2大匙
鹽 1¼小匙

太白粉 3大匙
水 4大匙

蛋(打散) 2個

🐟   🐟   🐟

12 medium shelled shrimp
3 fresh scallops (or fish fillet)
8 large clams

1 can creamed corn
5 c. stock or water
2 T. cooking wine
1¼ t. salt

3 T. cornstarch
4 T. water

2 eggs, beaten

🐟   🐟   🐟

12 camarones medianos pelados
3 escalopes frescos (o filete de pescado)
8 almejas grandes

1 lata elote cremoso
5 tz. caldo o agua
2 C. vino para cocinar
1¼ c. sal

3 C. maicena
4 C. agua

2 huevos, batidos

1 蝦仁去腸泥，鮮貝切薄片，大蜆吐沙後洗淨外殼。

2 將 **2** 料燒開，隨入 **1** 料再燒滾，以調勻的 **3** 料攪拌成薄汁，再燒開後淋入打散的蛋汁，使其散開即成。

☐ 如是用粿粒狀玉米罐頭，**3** 料內的太白粉需用5½大匙。

🐟   🐟   🐟

1 Devein shrimp. Slice fresh scallop into thin pieces. Allow clams to release sand then scrub clams clean.

2 Bring **2** to boil. Add **1**; return to boil. Stir in mixture **3**; stir and cook until thickened. Add beaten eggs when boiling; stir to separate the flakes.

☐ If canned whole kernel corn is used, increase the cornstarch in **3** to 5 1/2 T.

🐟   🐟   🐟

1 *Desvene los camarones. Rebane los escalopes frescos en rebanadas delgadas. Deje que las almejas suelten la arena luego talle y lávelas bien.*

2 *Haga hervir **2** . Agregue **1** ; vuelva a hervir. Agregue la mezcla **3** ; revuelva y cocine hasta que espese. Agregue los huevos batidos cuando esté hirviendo; revuelva para separar los pedazos.*

☐ *Si usa elote de grano entero enlatado, aumente la maicena de **3** a 5 1/2 C.*

MORE FROM WEI-CHUAN PUBLISHING

COOKBOOKS :

ALL COOKBOOKS ARE BILINGUAL (ENGLISH/CHINESE) UNLESS FOOTNOTED OTHERWISE

Apetizers, Chinese Style
Chinese Appetizers & Garnishes
Chinese Cooking, Favorite Home Dishes
Chinese Cooking For Beginners (Rev.)[1]
Chinese Cooking Made Easy
Chinese Cuisine
Chinese Cuisine-Cantonese Style
Chinese Cuisine-Shanghai Style
Chinese Cuisine-Szechwan Style
Chinese Cuisine-Taiwanese Style
Chinese Dim Sum
Chinese Herb Cooking for Health
Chinese Home Cooking for Health
Chinese One Dish Meals (Rev.)[3]
Chinese Snacks (Rev.)
Favorite Chinese Dishes
Fish[3]

Great Garnishes
Healthful Cooking
Indian Cuisine
International Baking Delights
Japanese Cuisine
Low Cholesterol Chinese Cuisine
Mexican Cooking Made Easy[4]
Noodles, Chinese Home-Cooking
Noodles, Classical Chinese Cooking
One Dish Meals; From Popular Cuisines[3]
Rice, Chinese Home-Cooking
Rice, Traditional Chinese Cooking
Shellfish[3]
Simply Vegetarian
Thai Cooking Made Easy
Vegetarian Cooking

SMALL COOKBOOK SERIES

Beef[2]
Chicken[2]
Soup! Soup! Soup!
Tofu! Tofu! Tofu!
Vegetables[2]
Very! Very! Vegetarian!

VIDEOS

Chinese Garnishes I[5]
Chinese Garnishes II[5]
Chinese Stir-Frying: Beef[5]
Chinese Stir-Frying: Chicken[5]
Chinese Stir-Frying: Vegetables[5]

OTHERS

Carving Tools

1 Also available in English/Spanish, French/Chinese, and German/Chinese
2 English and Chinese are in separate editions
3 Trilingual English/Chinese/Spanish edition
4 Also available in English/Spanish
5 English Only

Wei-Chuan Cookbooks can be purchased in the U.S.A., Canada and twenty other countries worldwide
1455 Monterey Pass Road, #110, Monterey Park, CA 91754, U.S.A. • Tel: (213)261-3880 • Fax: (213) 261-3299

味全叢書

食譜系列

(如無數字標註,即為中英對照版)

美味小菜
拼盤與盤飾
實用家庭菜
實用中國菜(修訂版)[1]
速簡中國菜
中國菜
廣東菜
上海菜
四川菜

台灣菜
飲茶食譜
養生藥膳
養生家常菜
簡餐專輯(修訂版)[3]
點心專輯
家常100
魚[3]
盤飾精選

健康食譜
印度菜
實用烘焙
日本料理
均衡飲食
墨西哥菜[4]
麵,家常篇
麵,精華篇
簡餐(五國風味)[3]

米食,家常篇
米食,傳統篇
蝦、貝、蟹[3]
健康素
泰國菜
素食

味全小食譜

牛肉[2]   湯
雞肉[2]   豆腐
蔬菜[2]   家常素食

錄影帶

盤飾 I[5]   炒菜入門,牛肉[5]
盤飾 II[5]   炒菜入門,雞肉[5]
                 炒菜入門,蔬菜[5]

其他

雕花刀

1 中英、英西、中法、中德版   2 中文版及英文版   3 中、英、西對照版   4 英文版   5 英文版

味全食譜在台、美加及全球二十餘國皆有發行 • 味全出版社有限公司 • 台北市仁愛路4段28號2樓
Tel:(02)2702-1148 • Fax:(02)2704-2729

OTROS LIBROS DE WEI-CHUAN

EDICIONES EN ESPAÑOL

Cocina China Para Principiantes, Edición Revisada[1]
Cocina Popular de Un Solo Platillo[2]
Comida China de Un Solo Platillo, Edición Revisada[2]
Comida Mexicana, Fácil de Preparar[3]
Mariscos, Estilo Chino Fácil de Preparar[2]
Pescado, Estilo Chino Fácil de Preparar[2]

1 Disponible en Inglés/Español, Inglés/Chino, Francés/Chino, y Alemán/Chino
2 Edición trilingüe Inglés/Chino/Español
3 Disponible en ediciones bilingües Inglés/Español e Inglés/Chino

Los Libros de Cocina Wei-Chuan se pueden comprar en E.E.U.U., Canadá y otros 20 países a través del mundo.
1455 Monterey Pass Road, #110, Monterey Park, CA 91754, U.S.A. • Tel: (213)261-3880 • Fax: (213) 261-3299